Troll Wall

Tony Howard

Troll Wall

Tony Howard

VERTEBRATE PUBLISHING

Vertebrate Publishing, Sheffield
www.v-publishing.co.uk

Troll Wall
Tony Howard

VERTEBRATE PUBLISHING
Crescent House, 228 Psalter Lane, Sheffield, S11 8UT
www.v-publishing.co.uk

First published in 2011 by Vertebrate Publishing, an imprint of Vertebrate Graphics Ltd.

This book is a work of non-fiction based on the life, experiences and recollections of
Tony Howard. The author has stated to the publishers that, except in such minor respects not
affecting the substantial accuracy of the work, the contents of the book are true.

A CIP catalogue record for this book is available from the British Library.

ISBN 978-1-906148-28-7

The paper used for this book is FSC-certified and
totally chlorine-free. FSC (the Forest Stewardship
Council) is an international network to promote
responsible management of the world's forests.

10 9 8 7 6 5 4 3 2 1

Typeset in Caslon by Vertebrate Graphics Ltd, Sheffield.
www.v-graphics.co.uk

Printed and bound in Malta on behalf of Latitude Press Ltd.

To the Trolls,
for letting us win.

And to the rest of the team, Bill, John, Nick, Rob, Jeff and Maggie,
also Smiler for his good company on the winter recce, to our patron,
Jack Longland, President of the British Mountaineering Council,
and Alan Baker, 'our man in London' for liaising with sponsors
and our many sponsors for making it possible.

I've come so oft to desperate grips
With Trolldom's power
God help the man whose foothold slips
In such an hour.

Arne Garborg

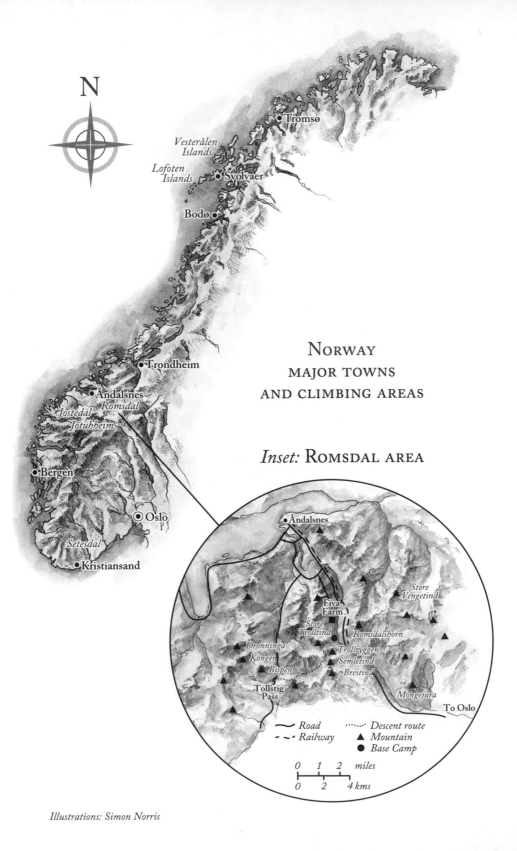

N

Tromsø

Vesterålen
Islands

Lofoten
Islands
Svolvær

Bodø

NORWAY
MAJOR TOWNS
AND CLIMBING AREAS

Trondheim

Åndalsnes
Romsdal

Jostedal
Jotuhheim

Inset: ROMSDAL AREA

Bergen

Oslo

Setesdal

Kristiansand

Åndalsnes

Fiva
Farm

Store
Vengetind

Store
Trolltind

Romsdalshorn

Dronninga
Kongen
Bispen

Trollryggen
Semletind
Breitind

Tollstig
Pass

Mongejura

To Oslo

—— Road   ⋯⋯⋯ Descent route
– – Railway   ▲ Mountain
                 ● Base Camp

0   1   2   miles

0   2   4 kms

Illustrations: Simon Norris

CONTENTS

FOREWORD

IT IS SOMEWHAT TYPICAL OF Tony Howard and the era when he did his greatest climbs that in 1965 he should write a comprehensive and, as it turns out, riveting account of his epic ascent of Troll Wall, then escape to the hills to avoid the limelight and forget all about it for nearly half a century. How wonderful that we can now read about the life and times of all the characters involved in this gripping Norwegian saga.

It is about time we had more information about this mountaineer, who has contributed so much to climbing here in Britain and abroad. This is a good, honest account, without exaggeration or too much understatement. Once begun, I found his account compulsive reading, a real page-turner, not just for those interested in big-wall climbing, but also for anyone who enjoys reading of epic journeys into the unknown.

The climbing of the Troll Wall by members of the Rimmon Mountaineering Club was significant in many respects. First, it brought into focus a new major area for big walls on a par with the Dolomites and Yosemite, albeit with a character all its own, affected by the cold moist winds blowing in from the North Sea. And the climb itself was an important development by virtue of the difficulties encountered and the commitment required to surmount them.

Of the seven Rimmon members on the Troll Wall expedition Rob Holt, Jeff Heath and Margaret Woodcock were there in support of the more experienced John Amatt, Tony Howard, Tony Nicholls and Bill Tweedale who planned to set off up the most natural line on the wall, straight up the centre with no possibility of escape other than up or back the way they had come.

This was a line Tony had previously reconnoitred. It captured their imagination and became their obsession. Their enthusiasm grew as they worked hard back in the UK to fund the expedition. The northern climbing scene had changed appreciably after the war.

Climbing abroad was no longer the preserve of the Alpine Club or Oxbridge types. During the 1960s and 1970s many local club expeditions were launched to faraway places, the Oread of Derby went to the Lyngen Peninsula of Arctic Norway and to Kulu in the Indian Himalaya. The Nottingham Climbing Club went to the Tibesti Mountains of Chad and the Hindu Kush of Afghanistan, and so on.

Now anyone with initiative could take advantage of the increased affluence and ease of travel, which became far cheaper too. It was no longer unusual for young climbers to work for eight months and then take the remainder of the year off climbing, hitchhiking out to the Alps, supplementing the tax rebate with casual work on building sites or, in the case of the Rimmon, on North Sea trawlers.

Ironically, after all those millennia left in the shadows since emerging from the last Ice Age, the Troll Wall saw the arrival of two separate groups in the same week, one from Norway and one from the north of England. The media had a field day and concocted the idea of 'a race' to be the first up the Wall.

What concerned Tony and his team when they heard of this 'race' was not they would be beaten to the top of the Wall but that they may not be first up 'their' route. They would not be the first to go where no-one had gone before, with all the intrinsic interest of discovery, the hidden cracks and ledges for belay and bivouac and the unravelling of the mysteries on this part of the mountain. That can only be experienced once, for once it is done and known there is no longer that compulsive curiosity that keeps a team on course through horrendous storms up exposed rock at great technical difficulty. Another Lancashire lad, Don Whillans, acknowledged that 'there has always been competition in climbing, but for the route, not to be better than anyone else.'

This was borne out subsequently when the Norwegians and Brits both succeeded in putting up two parallel and independent routes to the mutual admiration of both teams and although the Norwegians, as it happened, completed their route first they received whole-hearted congratulations from Tony, John and Bill and the rest of the Rimmon team. It mattered not a jot that the Norwegians were first up the Wall. In fact, as far as the Rimmon team were concerned, it was fitting that the Norwegians topped out first. It was 'their' mountain.

In the course of time the 'English Route' was recognised as a classic climb and became ever more popular. The Norwegian Route was not repeated until 1997 and only two or three times since. The Trolls had the last laugh, however, when the central part of the English Route peeled off in a massive avalanche. It has not been climbed since.

In taking on the challenge of the Troll Wall, the Rimmon lads took a huge step into the unknown. This was quite beyond anything any of them had attempted before. Consequently, the outcome remained uncertain until the end, which is always the hallmark of a great adventure. Modern climbers will find it hard to imagine how it was back in the 1960s on a 1,200-metre route surmounting huge overhanging sections, lashed by rain and sleet, climbing without harnesses, waterproofs and bivouac equipment, without 'portaledges', belay and abseil devices, pulley systems, or the modern protection we now take for granted.

They didn't take walkie-talkies so as not to 'rob the climb of the essence of being there alone and committed' and were therefore reliant upon their own judgement as to the weather, route finding and for each other's physical and psychological well-being.

It's true it wasn't an alpine-style ascent. They had cut down the odds against failure a little. Fixed polypropylene rope was employed on the lower approach slabs. The team did have to retreat when their bivouac gear failed in a prolonged storm leaving gear and food at their high point for a later attempt. They also had a few bolts, but didn't use them.

Tony Nicholls had led some of the hardest pitches on the first attempt and a done lot of sack hauling without a pulley. He was exhausted and with damaged hands decided he would only be a burden on the others so opted to stay down with the support party.

The other three had to adjust to their depleted team and the sadness at leaving a good mate behind.

Nowadays, it is not always appreciated that pegging is vastly different to bolting. Climbing up an overhanging wall for the first time, even with 280 pegs and wedges was never a foregone conclusion. If, however, the climbers resort to bolting, then with perseverance there is no doubt progress can be made. Drilling, therefore, really does 'murder the impossible.' Pegging, on the other hand, depends on the configuration of the crack systems. Progress is governed by the geography of the mountain and the climber's chances are restricted to using what features are available. Tony's description of negotiating the final part of the Great Wall shows pegging is not without risk and uncertainty. Only by stretching his strength, resourcefulness, imagination and courage to the limit could it be climbed even on pegs. Would today's climber armed with a battery operated drill have struggled so hard to avoid drilling? To have done so would have robbed the climb of its essence and diminished the great effort it was.

This section required great determination from all three of the team to hang throughout the night from their belays and etriers. Three days later, they reached the top of the Trollveggen to complete their odyssey. The climb opened up many possibilities for the Rimmon lads and for climbers everywhere, especially in Britain. The Troll Wall climb demonstrated what could follow from a ground-ing in British and Alpine rock and ice climbing. Local climbing clubs launched trips to the remote mountains of Alaska, Patagonia, Baffin Island and the Himalaya. Within ten years much harder, longer, steeper and higher routes were being established up in the Karakoram and Himalaya. By then climbers had the benefit of all the latest American climbing hardware and the software the Troll Climbing Equipment Company produced, the company started by Tony and two other members of the Rimmon Club, Paul Seddon and Alan Waterhouse. Perhaps the most important factor was the more rapid dissemination of information with climbers knowing far more, and more quickly, about other climbers' achievements everywhere.

In 1967, John Amatt, with Rusty Baillie, armed with skyhooks, rurps and the complete range of American hard steel pegs as well as bongs, climbed the 1,650-metre North Wall of Semletind in alpine style. John went on to become an accomplished public speaker and motivational lecturer. He emigrated to Canada where he established the Banff Mountain Film Festival.

Tony also continued, with other members of the Rimmon Club, to contribute, with a host of new climbs and the first walking and climbing guide to Romsdal. With Bill Tweedale, in 1967, he made the first ascent of Breitind's 2,000-metre East Pillar, and the equally long Pillar of Semletind with Rob Holt and Wayne Gartside. Tony, Bill, Rob and Wayne also climbed the 1,800-metre South East Face of Kongen.

Working as designer at Troll, Tony developed the world's first sit harness and later the Whillans harness. The lightweight version is, in the opinion of many, still the best mountain harness around. The day to day running of Troll was often largely left in the hands of Tony's co-directors, such was the call of the wild.

Tony, with his partner Di Taylor, discovered one new climbing and trekking area after another, in Morocco, Egypt, Ethiopia, the Sudan, Madagascar, Nagaland, Oman and, in particular, the Wadi Rum in Jordan. As a result of explorations there by Tony and his friends, and the guidebook Tony produced, Wadi Rum has become among the most popular desert climbing areas anywhere.

Dubbed with affection 'Howard of Arabia' by his friends, his title was confirmed when he brought out a walking guide to the hills of Palestine. It wasn't a best-seller but a plucky effort in view of the troubles afflicting Palestine then and since. In all the places Tony climbed he showed enormous respect for the environment and the local people, never more so than in Norway all those years ago.

Doug Scott, Cumbria
January 2011

'The Trolltind Wall is probably the highest sheer precipice in Europe, partly overhanging, and first mentioned in print in an article in the Alpine Journal about the highest mountain walls in the world. No one has ever tried the Trolltind wall – it looks too awful for ordinary climbers to aim at. There seem to be few places for resting on the wall and I have no hope that it is possible by normal mountaineering. However, as this is the most interesting and chief question among European climbers today, it is wholly worth a trial.'

Arne Randers Heen, Romsdal resident and the elder statesman of Norwegian mountaineering, in a letter to the author prior to the expedition.

Preface

In May 2010 I was asked by Dave Durkan, who was gathering information on Norwegian climbing history for the Norwegian Alpine Club, if I had any unpublished articles on the Troll Wall and my other climbs in Norway in the 1960s. Searching through old files, my partner, Di Taylor, found the faded, typed foolscap draft for this book. Written immediately after the climb, it was put to one side as other projects took over. I became involved in a lecture tour, wrote a guidebook and began forming Troll Climbing Equipment to market the gear we had designed for our ascent.

Then I was invited to crew a yacht sailing from Majorca to England. Soon afterwards I joined lads from our climbing club on a trip to Iceland. Following two hard winter months on the Icelandic trawlers, two of us then worked our passage to Norway on a small Danish cargo boat. This came close to sinking when the steering broke in a Force Eleven just off the cliffs of the Norwegian coast, but we arrived in Romsdal in time for the New Year festivities, staying there until the following autumn, doing new climbs and living, for the most part, off our trawling money supplemented through the summer by guiding. By then two years had passed since writing this book, more adventures beckoned and it stayed on its shelf, mostly forgotten. Forty-five years later, half a lifetime, and thanks to Dave, I rediscovered the manuscript, written by my younger self. What I read took me back to another world, an altogether different climbing era, and what had been a great first ascent. It seemed to me to have all the freshness and enthusiasm of a youthful adventure. I hope you feel the same. To give our climb some context, necessary after almost half a century, I've added an introduction and expanded the start of the book to include some of my relevant adventures in the Arctic and Antarctic. I've also added a postscript. Otherwise, it's as I wrote it, all those years ago.

The Troll Wall. At over 4,000 vertical feet, Europe's tallest rock face. *Photo: Tony Howard*

INTRODUCTION

As ROBERT SERVICE, great bard of the Klondike said, 'There are strange things done in the midnight sun.' The 1965 ascent of the Troll Wall in Norway, Europe's land of the midnight sun, by a bunch of unknown English lads was undoubtedly one of them. The Troll Wall was known as 'The Vertical Mile' and Europe's biggest unclimbed north face. It was also said to be impossible.

Our ascent took place in a different epoch as far as climbing goes. Equipment in the early 1960s had only just begun to develop from that used by the Victorian pioneers. True, their heavy hemp ropes had been replaced by stronger and lighter nylon following the successful British Everest Expedition in 1953 – the year I started climbing. Nailed boots had also rapidly vanished from the scene in the mid 1950s, being replaced by Vibram rubber. New lightweight climbing footwear was just coming onto the market. But climbing – especially leading – was still a bold undertaking with little in the way of leader protection. There were no belay devices. You held the rope in your hands and around your waist. There were also no abseil devices. You wound the rope around your body and slid down it, which was uncomfortable and quite dangerous. There were no comfortable portaledges for spending the night on big walls, nor had the great variety of American hard steel pegs arrived in the UK. The only pegs we had were soft steel that bent or crumpled if they met any obstacles when hammered into cracks. Jumar rope ascenders were also unavailable in the UK. We had the European version, Heibeler Prusiks, which were awkward to use and had a reputation for popping off ropes when in use, so we only carried them for emergencies.

Perhaps most surprisingly, there were no harnesses. The rope was simply tied round the waist or fastened to a waist-cord by a screw carabiner, made, like most carabiners at that time, not from aluminium alloy, but out of heavy steel with a thumb-tearing tooth in its gate. A rack of steel carabiners was almost as much a handicap as a necessity but luckily alloy crabs were just coming onto the market. And while we had pegs, they were considered unethical in Britain. Though their use had long been acceptable in the Alps and Dolomites, there was almost no aid climbing in Britain until the 1960s, when climbers began to develop their aid-climbing skills on overhanging limestone cliffs in Derbyshire and the Yorkshire Dales. Such places were, in those days, beyond the abilities of free-climbers. Even then, pegs were generally taboo on other climbs and rarely used.

Back in the early 1950s, when I started climbing, the only leader protection was via rope slings, the knots of which were sometimes jammed in cracks. Or else the slings themselves were hung on spikes of rock, or threaded round chockstones, which were sometimes carried up by the leader and inserted in cracks. By the end of that decade, the great innovation was old engineering nuts in various sizes that were threaded onto slings for jamming in cracks.

Special 'nuts' manufactured by climbers and designed purely for climbing only started to appear in the early 1960s, along with the lightweight alloy carabiners. The myriad shapes, styles and sizes of alloy wedges or 'nuts' on wire hadn't yet been dreamt of. Cams weren't produced until the late 1970s. The only protection in the wet, off-width, overhanging Exit Cracks of the Troll Wall were heavy and bulky wooden wedges that we had cut from the birch trees down at our Base Camp and carried all the way up the climb. The maxim of the day was still the same as it ever was: 'The leader never falls.'

Amongst these equipment pioneers were Alan Waterhouse, Paul Seddon and myself, all members of the Rimmon Mountain-eering Club, one of the many new clubs that sprang up in and around the Peak District at this time, such as the Manchester Grit, the Black and Tans, the Nottingham CC and the Alpha. The Rimmon were particularly active on northern gritstone, working on a new British Mountaineering Council guidebook to the Chew Valley. In 1963, they put up fifty-two new climbs on the remote cliff of Ravenstones in one day. Dave Cook later wrote in his article True Grit for *Mountain* magazine: 'There was a time in the late 1960s when it looked as if the ethos and traditions of gritstone were taking over everywhere. The big jamming fists, and the big jammed mouths of the Rock and Ice, the Alpha, the Black and Tans, the YMC and the Rimmon, proselytised by word and deed all over Britain brainwashing everyone else into an acceptance of inferiority.'

I was also doing a lot of aid climbing at the time, both on summer trips to the Dolomites and on Derbyshire's recently discovered overhangs, soloing routes such as *Big Plum*, *Avernus* and most of the first pitch of *Mecca*, whilst waiting for my late-sleeping climbing partner to arrive. Bob Dearman hung just a few feet away shouting encouragement as he worked on the first ascent of *The Prow*. The skills developed on these routes were, I suppose, partly responsible for giving me the confidence to attempt the Troll Wall. Aid-climbing also gave me the motivation to design a broad waist belt, both for the added comfort but also as a means of carrying gear. With a sling to form a seat, held in place by the belt, it made hanging around under big roofs, carrying gear, falling off and abseiling much more comfortable. And as I was mostly unemployed at that time, I could also earn a few quid making them for Bob Brigham to sell in his Manchester shop.

After the Troll Wall climb, this harness arrangement was successfully marketed as the Mark 2, before it was superseded five years later. By then, Alan, Paul and myself were partners in Troll Climbing Equipment. Working with Don Whillans, we came up with the design for the world's first true sit-harness – The Whillans – manufactured for the 1970 British Annapurna South Face Expedition. Another nine years were to pass before the best features of the Mark 2 and The Whillans were combined to form the Mark 5, a system linking a waist belt and leg loops with a front belay loop. This rapidly became the norm for almost all climbing harnesses. Troll also pioneered sewn tape slings, another important innovation. But ignorance is bliss, and in 1965 we were more than happy with our Mark 2 belts and our knotted slings on the Troll Wall.

Outdoor clothing and equipment was similarly primitive in the 1960s compared with today's sophisticated products. Lightweight fabrics used for waterproof clothing and the bivouac tents we designed for use on the Troll Wall were only marginally waterproof and definitely not breathable. Their failures led to our retreat from our first attempt at the climb. We were also acutely aware that rescue equipment was cumbersome and rudimentary. A rescue from high on the Troll Wall would have been a desperate, if not impossible, undertaking.

All these factors meant the wall was a huge challenge and a bold undertaking, far exceeding anything any of us had done previously. More experienced climbers than us advised us against attempting it, which was undoubtedly good advice. But we had the brash confidence of youth and it was waiting to be climbed. My maxim then as now was simple: 'You never know until you go.'

The Norwegian and British press had a field day. We were the 'The Magnificent Seven', aiming 'to beat the impossible north wall', variously described as anything from 3,000 to 6,000 feet. When it turned out that a team of Norwegian climbers were already at the foot of the wall when we arrived, the press were ecstatic. Their reports on the so-called 'race for the top' through 'fog hazard' and a 'blinding blizzard' which 'beat British team's bid' before we returned to 'inch up wall' then 'vanish in mist' until 'an observer saw a red thing creeping over the summit' were both unexpected and hilarious. Sometimes they were total fantasy. I have used extracts from some of these reports throughout the book.

The newspapers sensationalised the hazards and difficulties we encountered, bordering at times on the surreal. One reported how 'from their bivouacs [the climbers] watched huge boulders drift away in the wind' – a rather bizarre image. This tendency to exaggerate the experiences of climbers is commented on by Simon Thompson in his book *Unjustifiable Risk? The Story of British Climbing*, when he writes that a certain 'Donald Robinson, who died in a climbing accident in 1910, observed that a truly honest account of a climbing day has yet to be written.' Thompson goes on to say that that 'there are only two approaches to writing about climbing: exaggeration and understatement.' This story is neither, I hope. Understatement may be a peculiarly English trait and is certainly common among climbers, but in telling the story of this climb, I tried to tell an honest tale while it was still fresh in my mind. Accounts of other climbs in this book were also written immediately afterwards.

We named our climb the Rimmon Route, but it also became known internationally as the English Route. With all pegs left in place and more added by subsequent climbers, it became the most popular climb on the wall. John Middendorf and Aslak Aastorp described it as being 'a masterpiece of route finding at the highest free and aid standards of the day.' Even so, with its fabled invincibility gone, and as equipment and climbing standards improved, it was inevitably climbed free of aid as well as being soloed and climbed in winter.

Sadly, the Rimmon Route became an early victim of global warming when permafrost within the mountain melted, causing the centre of the face to fall away in a huge rockfall in 1998. The section of our climb from above the Great Wall up to and including the Narrow Slab was lost, along with pitches of other more recent routes on this part of the face.

Tony Howard, Greenfield, on the northern edge of the Peak District January 2011

PART ONE

A Very
Norwegian Saga

One

Antarctic Adventures

'The chief harpoonist, a Norwegian of massive build… recalled the frustration of the storms they had had at the start of the season. It was impossible to hunt in that sort of weather. You could never spot the whale spouts because of the spindrift, and anyway the bow dipped too violently to aim the harpoon gun. For long stretches they had to shelter in the lee of an iceberg; a week once went by without a "Bluust!" ("There she blows!") He personally had bagged 323 whales this time and only two of them were blues. He was pretty sure they were disappearing.'

From **The Observer** on a voyage of the Southern Venturer in 1962

MY PERSONAL NORWEGIAN SAGA started in 1958, the year I left school, and it took me first not to Norway but to the Antarctic. Our headmaster at Oldham Hulme Grammar lined us up in the school hall at the end of our final term. 'And where do you intend to continue your studies,' he asked each boy as he walked down the row: 'Oxford, Sir, reading History'; 'Cambridge, Sir, reading Physics.' Then it was my turn: 'The Antarctic, Sir, going whaling.' It felt wildly exciting, even anarchic. Who could resist?

My poor father wasn't at all happy with my decision, but my uncle had a contact in the Norwegian whaling business and at my request had fixed me up as a mess boy on the Southern Venturer, a name to conjure up dreams of Antarctic exploration in a seventeen-year-old boy. 'We should let him go,' Mum said. 'If we do, he'll never settle down', my father replied, prophetically as it turned out. The concept of a 'gap year' didn't exist in the 1950s; for those that made the grade, university followed on from school and that's how it was. Unluckily for Dad, it had been him that had encouraged my wanderlust with his books of adventure in the far corners of the British Empire. He had also introduced me to the hills, walking the moors of the northern Peak District with me in my pre-teens and a couple of times seeing climbers on cliffs like Laddow, a rare event even though Laddow was popular at the time.

After that I used to dream about climbing, playing around on boulders up the Chew Valley with my mates and one day at the age of thirteen, finding a guidebook below the cliffs of Alderman, the nearest thing we had to a mountain. Not being aware that guidebooks even existed, this discovery changed everything. I discovered that my home hills were full of recorded cliffs and climbs and that my friends and I had even done some of the easier routes without knowing. After this there was no going back. I never settled down to serious study, preferring the hills and crags to schoolwork. The chance of an Antarctic adventure was too much to resist.

Being born into a poor family, Dad never had the chance to go to university, and had to leave the same school that I went to, to earn a living, despite having good qualifications. Now here I was following in his footsteps but about to squander the opportunity he had valued so highly. But Mum won the day. She knew it was important to follow your dreams and, in October 1958, now aged eighteen, I boarded the Southern Venturer, bunking in a cabin with a lad of my age from Newcastle who had also signed on as a mess boy, and sailing to Norway to pick up most of the crew. Then we sailed south. Before long the ship's doctor spotted my A-level credentials and asked if I would like to join him and his assistant in the ship's hospital. This sounded better than serving food in the mess and washing pots, so I happily accepted.

You may wonder what on earth I was doing on a whaler. Had I no ethics? Didn't I care about whales nearing extinction? I won't make excuses, but it was, back then, a different world. No one thought the seas might be fished out within fifty years. No one thought whales were nearing extinction. The International Whaling Commission was in charge. They decided the permissible catch: how many sperm whales, how many fin, humpback and blue. Not only that but the ship's captain wasn't informed which species of whale could be hunted, and how long for, until the day before, so everything was okay – or so I thought. And yes, it was bloody and cruel, and on occasion the ocean ran red with blood, but for an eighteen-year-old lad fresh from school, it was life in the raw, the life of the hunter, of *Moby Dick*. But when Greenpeace began its campaign against whaling in 1975, I joined immediately. I had seen the slaughter.

When Greenpeace began its campaign against whaling in 1975, I joined immediately. I had seen the slaughter. *Photo: Tony Howard*

The crew was predominantly Norwegian, most of them from the far north, including the Lofoten and Vesterålen islands, with a fair scattering of Scots from the Shetlands, Orkneys and Hebrides. They were tough but friendly, hard-working men, always ready with a joke, and for most this was an annual trip to the southern whaling grounds. There were very few English, so I picked up a bit of Norwegian and discovered that there were impressive mountains in Norway's Arctic north, giving me the idea of a climbing trip up there, though I soon had my own little mountain adventure in South Georgia, where we docked for a few days. Just the mention of its name filled my mind with thoughts of an island lashed by storms and filled with majestic peaks of snow and ice. I knew the tales of Shackleton and his great adventure. South Georgia was an island fortress guarding the gateway to the Antarctic and the unknown. Now I was in the whaling station of Leith Harbour, surrounded by those very mountains. My equipment was poor, consisting of an old anorak and sweater, a pair of fancy rather than functional trousers, and an old pair of 'kletterschuhe', a 1950s version of the modern lightweight hillwalking boot. This was hardly the gear for glacier travel.

Even so, with a day free, I set out 'just to have a look' at Glacier Peak. This was the most prominent peak in the immediate vicinity of the bay where we were docked, with a rock ridge circling northwards round the glacier to Corunda Peak above the harbour. Within half an hour I was at the foot of the glacier, feeling very small, and apprehensive. This was my first glacier, yet the temptation to climb it and try to climb Glacier Peak by a ridge that, as far as I knew, was unclimbed felt irresistible. Why couldn't I just walk round the valley and look from afar? My gear was non-existent and I knew as much about snow and ice climbing as I did about space travel.

Fooling myself that I would just go up a bit and stop at any danger, I set off up the glacier, which rose pleasantly towards the summit ridge, then levelled off to an area of deep crevasses and ice seracs. Impressed, I sat down to ponder the situation. The view was superb. Across the valley a rock face rose steeply for about fifteen hundred feet, seamed with gullies that were rotting away onto the screes below. Above and beyond, thrusting like countless Excaliburs from a lake of clouds, were innumerable jagged peaks, their icy summits glistening and beckoning in the sunlight. I sat alone in the solitude of the mountains, until the cold of the glacier penetrated my trousers and I returned to the reality of my situation.

Inspired by my surroundings, I was in no mood for going down. I leapt happily across crevasses until suddenly – scrunch – my foot went through the snow. With a sickening feeling in my stomach I crawled rapidly onto safer terrain and once more sat down. Behind me a hole led the eye down into pitch blackness. This wasn't so good. Still, I reasoned, the day was yet young and with only another hundred feet or so of glacier and its final bergschrund to cross I could take my time and continue.

Beyond this last crevasse, the snow rose steeply and having jumped over, my rubber soled 'klets' didn't help at all. The snow was too hard for step kicking, and any attempt at jumping back would almost certainly have ended in the green-blue depths far below. The only way out was to scrape holds into the icy snow with my fingernails. This was tricky work, but I soon climbed high above the mouth of the bergschrund, with only a hundred feet of rock to the summit ridge. 'This is more like it,' I thought. 'It looks a bit loose, but at least it's rock.'

The rock wasn't just 'a bit' loose, it was actually collapsing. Block after tottering block littered the wall, interspersed by crumbling bands of shale. I eased along from hold to hold hoping that no more than one would give way at the same time. Then, after what seemed hours of suspense, there I was at last, sitting astride the crumbling knife-edge ridge.

'Thank God I'm up,' I thought, exceedingly impressed by myself and my amazing location. Beneath my right foot a shattered chaos of slabs swept down for about two thousand feet to a deep green sea, boiling and foaming white on the rocks. To my left was the face I had just climbed, the black hole of the bergschrund gaping like the mouth of a whale. Ahead and behind snaked a fantastic, impossible ridge of crazy pinnacles leading to the summits of Glacier and Corunda Peaks. The view and feeling of isolation were unforgettable. The only trouble was, just what happened next? There was no way I was going on that face again.

My only option was to move cautiously along the ridge then descend steep scree, which disappeared into the jaws of the bergschrund. 'Nasty,' I thought, 'but here goes.' And it did. Before I knew it, I was sliding helter-skelter, bottom-end down, straight towards the depths of who knows what. Those scree stones were sharp too. I remember thinking, 'I'd better do something about this quick, or I'm a goner.' As I reached the mouth of the bergschrund I pushed my legs out to bridge the gap. They just reached the lip of the glacier on the other side and I jammed myself across the crevasse. Stones rattled on into the icy blackness. Then all was silent. Laughing with relief, I decided that if I ever got down I'd give climbing up immediately.

Carefully unjamming myself, I slowly reached across and pulled over onto the glacier where I sat down with a sigh of relief, although not for long. The back of my trousers and the equivalent area of my bum had ceased to be. Instead there was a shredded mass of skin dripping blood onto the snow. This was disastrous. Not only did I have to descend the glacier and walk back down the valley with a torn arse, I also had to get back on board ship without looking like the fool I was. Never mind. With my anorak tied around my waist I was soon nonchalantly strolling up the gangplank trying my best to look like a hard mountaineer, but secretly feeling thankful to still be alive.

The following morning the ship left for the Antarctic whaling grounds. The mountains of South Georgia would be our last landfall for almost three months. For days I was given a painful reminder of its mountains every time I sat down. I never did stop climbing, but I did learn a lesson: fate sometimes favours the foolish.

The whaling was non-stop, broken only by the festivities of Christmas and Easter. For me, as a 'first-seasoner', life was constantly interesting. In addition to the whaling – the regular catches of sperm whale and fin, the three hundred humpback in three days, the awesome, gigantic blue whales, the largest animal our planet has ever seen – there was also my work in the ship's hospital. As well as keeping the surgery clean, or should I say ship-shape, I had to bring the doctor his meals from the galley at the bows of the ship, running the gauntlet of cables, flensing knives, whale blubber and the stinking, blood-covered deck. I also helped the doctor with all the usual industrial injuries, gashes and bruises. More excitingly, we had to perform a couple of appendectomies and one more serious operation. A guy had fallen from the crow's nest and was bleeding from internal injuries. It turned out he had a ruptured spleen. It was a long operation, for which the ship was stopped. I had to swab down the surgery until it was spotless, not really my forte, and help with the operation, mopping out the bloodbath of his chest cavity and watching the doctor massage his heart to resuscitate him when he seemed to be dying. I was also in charge of the numerous clips and other instruments, passing them to the doctor when needed and counting them in and out. 'Is that everything?' said the doc, when we finished. What a question. 'Yes,' I said hesitantly, hoping I hadn't got it wrong. This was serious stuff for a young lad.

Even so, I was missing the crags and the camaraderie of the climbing scene, as well as the girls, and was glad when the last whale was killed and we were able to start our return voyage from the icy waters off Antarctica's Enderby Land back to the rocky shores of South Georgia. In another month the southern winter would be starting and the iceberg-scattered seas through which we were sailing would freeze. Back home it would soon be spring and there were routes to be done.

Already, on the mountains above the whaling station at Leith Harbour where I had my unforgettable experience, there had been some snowfall. This time I managed to snatch a day off with a friend to wander a few miles along the coast of the island to the Norwegian whaling base of Stromness, which Shackleton had reached on foot over the mountains in 1916 with five of his men, making the first crossing of the unmapped interior of South Georgia's terra incognita. His polar quest had come to an end when his ship, The Endurance, was crushed by pack ice in October 1915. After drifting on an ice floe, they struggled to reach Elephant Island in three small boats, after which Shackleton and five other men sailed to the southern coast of South Georgia. From there, they crossed the mountains to raise a rescue, which sailed from the nearby whaling station of Grytviken. Shackleton was buried there in 1922, having died from a heart attack on his next Antarctic venture.

Beyond Stromness, whalebones littered the beach and penguins waddled clumsily down the rocks to drop as though suicidally into the crashing waves, then disappear like speeding torpedoes out to sea. Further along the beach, gigantic sea elephants lay idly in our path. We threaded our way somewhat nervously between them, at times only a few feet away. If we came too near any of the calves, the mother would raise her head to emit a horrible gurgling sound. Later that day, we passed a small sleek calf on its own by the water's edge. It stared at us timidly with large round eyes before sliding into the water leaving only a swirling eddy in its wake. Up above us, a hanging glacier descended from the tempting peak of Mount Paget, but the next day we were sailing for England. Given my previous experience, it was perhaps just as well.

Two

Arctic Adventures

'The vast mountain ranges of Norway provide an ideal playground for holiday makers. The scenery is truly magnificent – the giant peaks, glistening glaciers, remote mountain valleys, thundering waterfalls, peaceful lakes and blue fjords cutting deep into the mountain ranges... Although most peaks have been climbed there is certainly scope for further exploring... there are walls and ridges which will yield good sport, but which have never been climbed. The scope for new climbs of all standards of difficulty, particularly in Arctic Norway, is still considerable and several problems of a high order of difficulty remain.'
Per Prag, *Mountain Holidays in Norway*, 1963

Once home I appeased my father by holding down a job in a hospital pathology laboratory for a couple of years, cragging in the evenings on our local grit, and further afield at weekends and holidays. It wasn't to last. Working in a hospital, I was inevitably expected to work weekends. I couldn't do it. I quit work and left home, finding a cottage on the edge of the moors at ten bob a week. That's fifty pence in today's money, but at that time about two or three hour's pay if you were working, or a fifth of your dole money if, like me, you weren't. Somehow I saved enough to go to the Alps that summer. The Matterhorn was our objective, but the weather was foul. We climbed a few minor routes but nothing to satisfy. Then I remembered the whaler's stories of Arctic Norway and began searching for information. I discovered Per Prag's marvelous, inspirational paperback series, *Rock Climbs in Norway*, which were published in 1953 and later became part of his 1963 book *Mountain Holidays in Norway*. They were filled with pointers to unclimbed walls and even mentioned unclimbed peaks. The following summer, together with friends from the Rimmon Mountaineering Club and Manchester Gritstone Club, I headed for the islands of Lofoten and Vesterålen prospecting for new climbs.

It was our first expedition and a great trip, adventurous and fun, which for me is what it's always been about. Our primary objective was a mountain called Reka, 'The Spade', on the island of Langøy, which, it is said, was once inhabited by a gigantic troll.

Reka from Eidsfjord. *Photo: Alf Oxem*

He had been busy carving out the fjords that twist their way into and between the islands, and was digging a channel between Eidsfjorden and Skjerfjorden. The troll worked so hard through the night that he forgot about the clock, but trolls cannot live in sunlight, so as dawn was breaking he became so angry he threw the spade away. When the blade hit the ground, the handle broke, landing in the sea. The proof of the story is Bjørndalsfjorden, or Bear Valley Fjord, which forms the unfinished channel, Rekøya or Reka Island, the handle) and Reka, the spade, still thrusting out of the ground for all to see.

Despite Reka's meagre two thousand feet, it was described in the guide as 'the most impressive peak in Arctic Norway'. Its dimensions are so fine that it only presents two faces. They are separated by a narrow ridge, which rises sheer from the hillside in the north, to pass over the quarter-mile knife-edge summit and drop down overhangs to the south west. The north ridge is unclimbed, and the only means of descent is by abseiling down the overhangs of the south west ridge. The vertical eye-catching thousand-foot walls and corners of the south east face had never been attempted. Only the north west face had been climbed, and this in two places. The first ascent was up grooves of Diff standard in 1906, and the second by a rather harder line in 1958 climbed by Magnar Petterson and Arne Randers Heen – at that time, two of Norway's best known mountaineers. The third and almost unexpected ascent was made by us on the first night of June, 1962.

We had pitched our tents beneath the wall the previous day. Spring had yet to arrive; it had been a bad winter with twice the normal snowfall. The birch trees were still bare and the foot-thick ice on the lake, despite being only sixty feet above sea level, was only just beginning to break, splitting into a cobweb of cracks. Our intention was to circle Reka by some subsidiary ridges on the following day to get a closer view of its walls and ridges. The day after, we planned to do one of the recognised routes, and finally we hoped to attempt a new route on the south east face.

All this would, of course, depend on the weather, and even though we knew the winter had been particularly harsh, we thought it reasonable to assume conditions would improve by June.

Unfortunately we were wrong, as that very first night snow started to drift gently down. By the time we woke, the whole cirque of peaks was languishing peacefully under a thick mantle of snow and the black, harsh precipices of yesterday were no longer. It was a pleasant and restful scene, and always prone to suggestions of rest we curled up again in the warmth of our sleeping bags till two in the afternoon, brewing tea to pass the time. By then most of the night's snow had melted and we crept out to kindle up a good warm fire and have breakfast. In the land of the midnight sun, what does it matter when you get up? Norway is the perfect country for the idle alpinist.

We left our non-climbing member, Mick 'Chipperfield' Stevens, to guard camp and cook some stew up when he saw us returning, and set off later that afternoon. With our previous plan in mind, we traversed some small peaks to the base of the north ridge. From our viewpoint, the south east face presented a vertical silhouette, broken only by the occasional overhang and the dark slash of blade straight cracks. The north ridge still held a smattering of snow and was capped by a small overhang. Even so, we worked out a possible line, and a route should go there. To the right was the easier-angled section of the north west face, and the grooves of the 1906 route. Still following our programme, we glissaded down to the bottom of this wall with the intentions of traversing the snow slopes beneath, and so up to the south west col.

From a small rocky knoll protruding from the snow at halfway, we could view the face, and there, almost in the centre, was an obvious line of ascent – a gully down the steepest and highest part of the wall. We all saw it and each knew what the other was thinking, but who would suggest it? It was Jim Cooper, the eldest of us and a member of the Manchester Grit, who finally spoke and, of course, we all agreed. To hell with the plan, the route looked good and it should go. We searched the sacks for a few nuts and raisins, putting them with a few items of clothing, some pegs, a hammer and an axe into one sack to go with us, and leaving the rest to be collected later. Next, we roped into two teams and by ten that night we were on the face. The weather was good and the sun was hanging low over the horizon in a dull red glow.

Once across the small bergschrund, a series of ascending traverses brought us to a tricky pitch that led across the vertical wall into the narrow gully. This had rather more ice on its walls than we had expected and at its narrowest point was blocked by an ice-coated block, dripping with icicles, which proved particularly awkward. Above this, the steepening angle and amount of ice forced us to re-rope into a party of four and traverse out onto the slabs and grooves of the right wall. Up to this point, Jim and I, having the most experience of mixed rock and ice work, had been leading the two ropes. Now Jim came up to join me so that we could change leads if necessary. 'Jonah' – Tony Jones – our young rock wizard was next, then 'Harpic' Harold Heald, so called as he was 'clean round the bend', came a valiant fourth with the sack of gear and the axe, balancing up the verglassed slabs.

Six hundred feet up the face, we were forced into what looked like a complete impasse. The only approachable break was a sixty-foot hanging corner similar to the Flake Crack on *Central Buttress* on Scafell, but facing in the opposite direction. Its right wall leant out in a dark bulge over its vertical, ice-covered partner, but using two runners for aid I managed to reach a good chock just beneath what we hoped would be the final obstacle in this section. To continue up the next ten feet without pegs was obviously impossible in those conditions, so I rigged a seat up with a couple of slings on the chockstone and shouted down for the gear.

By this time it was midnight and the peaks to the north were crouching in a jumbled black mass against the pale glow of the North Atlantic reflecting the rays of the midnight sun. Moments later the sun disappeared from sight behind the wall, casting a dark shadow over the cliff. The cold of the Arctic night increased, and as I hauled up the axe and the jingling collection of pegs, we felt the first flakes of snow falling from grey clouds that had been gathering, almost unnoticed, for the past hour.

Anxious to escape the oppressive cold of the corner, I attempted to climb the overhang by chipping some steps in the black ice of the left wall, then bridging across. It was futile and rather hair-raising. Down below the others were waiting patiently, huddled on snow-covered ledges to escape the rising wind. I returned quickly to the overhang and fiddled amongst the pegs with cold fingers. There was a narrow crack cutting the bulge, and the first two pegs went in well, so I was able to swing up out of the corner. Down below, Jim took the strain on the rope as I tensioned out awkwardly to a crack on the right. It was choked with frozen earth and at a bad angle, but with no alternative, I hammered the third peg in and swung round. With the ropes dragging through the pegs and fingers raw with cold, I grasped at the snow-covered ledge above and pulled slowly up. I found a good belay and my fingers thawed out taking the rope in as the others followed, removing the pegs.

A strong wind was now blowing the snow across the face. With the sun hidden behind the mountains, the cold was intense. Jim took over the lead, and we went on up the wall following a further series of slabs until at eight hundred feet we reached the second big problem. Our line of ascent ended in a blank wall, and the next groove started some fifteen feet to the right across a steep, almost holdless, slab. We crouched together on a small ledge and nibbled at some chocolate and raisins. The cold wind and continuous effort were beginning to affect us all, and it would be up to Jonah to crack this next pitch, the key to the summit. Could he climb what amounted to a delicate gritstone problem in mountain boots and with frozen feet and fingers?

We re-roped with Jonah in the lead and he moved out onto the slab. After a few tentative attempts, it was obvious that the solution was a delicate mantelshelf, then a traverse into a groove.

He came back to warm his fingers up, and on the second attempt he made the move onto the icy hold. We watched anxiously, teeth chattering with the cold and snow, as he balanced perfectly across and then laybacked up into the groove. We followed in various ungainly styles and Jim led through onto a rib, which took us delightfully, despite the bitter conditions, to the final wall. It was eight in the morning.

Away to the west, the weak rays of the morning sun were now catching the snow-covered slopes of nearby peaks with their pale light, and the reflected glow cheered us with thoughts of the new day and returning warmth. Yet, with only fifty feet to go to the summit ridge, we were not to escape easily. The face still held one last problem, a twenty-foot ice-covered wall undercut at its base by a small overhang. It was sixteen hours since yesterday's late breakfast and none of us felt particularly fresh. With the added rigours of almost constant leading and route finding both Jim and I were grateful for Jonah's offer to try the final pitch.

Using a peg he passed the overhang, and balanced up onto some small holds. Above, he led on, bridging precariously on the ice-covered wall. He slipped once, managing to grasp a hold above at the last moment, before disappearing up the final slope. We followed quickly and by nine-thirty we were all four standing on the snow-plastered summit, lashed by the strong wind. We had been on the wall for almost twelve hours and the top was no place to linger.

Soaked to the skin, we descended the verglassed slabs of the south west ridge to the overhang where we were exposed to the full force of the Arctic blizzard. Glad that an abseil peg was already in place, marking the way, we threw the doubled rope over, to be caught in the grip of the wind, flailing in space. Whether it would reach the bottom or not, we couldn't tell, but Jim went over first and shouted everything was okay. The ends just reached. Below, the tortuous descent of the ridge continued into a haze of snow until eventually we reached the south west col and glissaded down into the comparative shelter of the face.

Our footsteps of yesterday were almost gone and snow had already begun to drift over our sacks. It took us a while to find them. Then we plunged down to the birch trees by the lake. There it was raining, but before we had gone far even this stopped and soon, across the grey ice of the lake, we could see our camp, and there was Chippie. We shouted and waved our axes furiously and, as we squelched on through the lakeside swamp, we saw the fire burst into life.

He handed us steaming mugs of tea. I could smell whale steaks, a gift from the locals, sizzling over the fire. We had been out for twenty-three hours on the mountain. Maybe it wasn't quite what we had planned, but it was certainly memorable. We followed this success with more first ascents on nearby summits despite the continuing bad weather, before taking a ferry over to the nearby island of Hinnøy where the hospitable Norwegians had arranged for us to borrow two rowing boats and offered the use of a cabin below the mountains as a Base Camp.

The cabin was approached up two lakes separated by a portage. This was hard work, even with four of us pushing and pulling at each boat as we sweated our way to the top of a hill to reach the second lake. Below us, the river roared over the falls from the upper lake to splash shallowly down over rounded stones and eventually lose itself in the calm waters of the lower one. The track rose up through birch trees now bursting into leaf, before opening out onto a grassy slope and the boulder-strewn shores of the upper lake.

Beyond, seeming to crouch defiantly at the head of the lake, and almost dwarfing Moisalen, the island's highest point, were the three peaks of the Raudtind, an impressive trio. Our attention was immediately caught by the ridge of the central peak, which snaked down the edge of the north face and plunged deep into the snowy recess of the corrie below. It seemed to present a beautiful line of ascent and probably the only one from this side of the mountain. We wondered why it hadn't been climbed.

As we rowed up the top lake to the hunting cabin, the ridge slowly presented itself in all its eye-catching detail, cast into silhouette by the rays of the sun, which formed a deep shadow on its overhanging south wall. Each tower of the ridge was capped by snow, and the summit itself had its own permanent snowfield, the heavy cornices of which hung in a grey curve over the two thousand foot slabs of the snow-splashed north face. The lower rocks were grey and worn smooth by the glaciers, but above rose wall upon wall of dull red rock split by ice-filled grooves and snow-covered ledges.

Even as we approached the hut, we could see and hear the avalanches, which were sweeping down this wall and those of the surrounding peaks. The black debris carried down by the snow rolled silently to a stop in the deep snow of the corries as the roar of the falls echoed across the lake. We didn't need a textbook to tell us that this was a time for sunbathing and fishing, whilst the summer sun removed the worst of winter's snows.

It was almost a fortnight later when two of us set out for what had become known to us as 'The Big Ridge'. The hanging walls of snow had receded and we had already had three splendid days on the needles and towers of the lakeside ridges, though Jonah was now grounded, recovering from an arm injury after being hit by a falling stone five hundred feet up an unclimbed face. The other two lads were making a trip over to the col at the head of the valley. As the excellent weather of the past week was beginning to break, this would probably be our last chance at an attempt so we had to take it.

An hour after leaving the hut, Harold and I were moving up the easy snow slopes of the corrie below the face. Lower down the hillside a trail of smashed and twisted birch saplings was mute evidence of the strength of the avalanches. Above us, small rivulets of water dripped and glistened down the wall and the summit snows gleamed white against the blue sky. To the left, the ridge dropped down to disappear into a small bergschrund emphasised sharply as a black gash above the snow.

Kicking steps up the slope, the snow was hard and crisp, bursting out from under our boots to hiss and trickle down the hillside.

We roped up and strode over the crevasse onto the rocks of the first tower and after some easy scrambling we were soon traversing a beautiful little knife-edge of snow, which ended all too abruptly at the second wall. We had never been more dismayed than we were at the bottom of that tower. It was obviously no place to be. Above us tottered three hundred feet of chaotic red rock shattered into a myriad splinters and hanging over space with a terrifying disregard for gravity. Our one thought was to get out of there. If we were going to continue, we would have to be doubly quick and extra safe. Timidly we tapped a peg in for a belay, afraid that the noise would bring the whole ruin of the tower down on us.

Eager to be on the move, I set off carefully in an ascending spiral towards a crackline we had seen from the hut with our binoculars. It lay between the crumbling rocks of the tower and the sweeping slabs of the north face, and I reached it after a hundred and fifty feet of nerve-wracking insecurity, with the rope knocking holds off at almost every move. By the side of the chimney was a small niche and sheltered by its projecting roof I tried to fix a belay, but every crack I tried with a peg simply opened up with the first knock. Eventually I had to manage with two poor pegs fastened in tension and Harold came gingerly round into the niche and clipped in. I went on again, following the comparative water-worn solidity of the chimney, which eased off onto a pleasant snow slope above what we had now named Hell Tower. Harold led on, and we continued by the side of a cornice curling out over the overhang of the south face to the base of the next obstacle, a vertical pinnacle-topped wall, which we named the Black Tower.

By the time we had chimneyed up to the top of the pinnacle the blue skies of the early morning had gone, and clouds were creeping in, feeling their way with cold, ghost-grey fingers across the rocks of the north face. The nearby peaks were already caught in their grasp and the lake was beginning to form white tipped waves as the wind increased. From far below we heard the enquiring shout of the other party returning from the col.

They stood, looking up, two small black specks on the distant snowfield and we called down, reassuring them that all was well.

Whilst they hurried on to the warmth and comfort of the hut, the first wind-blown drops of sleet began to lash their way over the face and we pulled on our duvets and fastened up the hoods. We would have to hurry. With almost a thousand feet still to go and more than that beneath us, this was no place to be caught in an Arctic storm. Leaving the pinnacle to get back onto the wall involved a hard move, and above this a series of zigzag traverses brought us to a bulging corner. It was running wet and streaked with verglas, so without further ado we brought out the pegs. There was no time to waste.

By standing on the third peg we had placed it was possible to pull up with the axe onto a small hanging snowfield, tilted at a precarious angle down the ridge. Behind was a small rock overhang that took a peg belay and I brought Harold up before swinging out and moving up onto the snow crest below the final Summit Tower. By now the wind was powering fiercely over the ridge, tearing at the mist and dashing icy, stinging sleet against us and the mountain. In the hope of a fast ascent, we wasted precious time and energy on a direct assault of this last wall, but with only five hundred feet to go, it proved impossible. Instead I traversed out onto the upper verglassed slabs of the north face, where the only weakness was an ice-filled groove that would need pegs. Hoping that the south wall would prove easier, I returned and went out to the left. Nothing doing. Not relishing the idea of a two thousand foot descent of the ridge, we decided on the pegs and once again managed with three.

Ahead rose the final splendid snow slope, providing us with some enjoyable step cutting, and just over the crest of the summit we found a sheltered hollow beneath the cornice and drank a glorious concoction of blueberry juice and sugar followed by oranges and raisins. The blustering wind slowly quietened and the snow no longer whirled madly around us, but drifted silently down to settle and melt on the dampness of our clothes. Even so, it was no place to relax, and as the grey clouds swirled and thinned in the corries below, we returned to the knife-edge summit ridge. To our right, the snow curved down sharply over the sweep of the north face and we stayed roped up as we descended by the rocks of the west ridge to a windswept col, before finishing with a glorious thousand foot glissade into the corrie beneath the wall.

Another three quarters of an hour took us back through the gently dripping trees to the river and the lake idly rocking the boats on the stones by the hut door. A curl of blue wood smoke rose from the chimney and disappeared into the clearing skies. From the half-open window came the sound of a guitar, whilst inside over the crackling fire, a bubbling stew boiled and steamed, sharpening our hunger. The lads helped us off with our wet gear and we changed into some warm clothes they had hung over the stove for us. We ate and talked about the climb well into the night. We had climbed 'The Big Ridge' and renamed it Rødklinge, The Red Blade; we had been given one more memorable mountain experience. The kettle sang on the stove and the midnight sun shone peacefully over the lake and the mountains. This was living.

A few days later we left for home, Jonah and I stopping off on the island of Austvagøy, where we unexpectedly met a couple of lads from the Swiss Alpine Club, Bruno Hoffman and Kurt Schneider. We sailed with them up the Raftsund in the local milk boat, visiting the fjord-side farms before disembarking and camping beneath the peaks of Trakta and Trolltind. The weather was superb and we climbed them in the following days, cooling off with a swim in the Gulf Stream-warmed Arctic water.

We also made what we discovered later was the first one-day traverse of the peaks, climbing overnight by the light of the midnight sun over the summits of Trakta, Store Trolltind and the three peaks of Trolltindmuren, completing the route in twelve hours. Almost fifty years on, many Norwegian climbers still consider Trakta the most difficult Alpine mountain in Norway with the easiest route at about British VS.

By this time Jonah and I were penniless and getting home became an adventure in itself, jumping ferries, working for food in hotels and cafés, sometimes being taken in and fed by farmers as we slowly hitched our way south, making sure we passed through Romsdal to get a look at the notorious Troll Wall, Europe's biggest north face and still unclimbed. Sadly it was concealed in mist and rain. It didn't occur to me then that in three years I would be climbing it.

Part Two

Troll Wall
Preparations

THREE

Reconnaissance

'Few tourist destinations in Norway have evoked more lyrical outbursts than Romsdal. The valley with its mountain ranges is said to be a worthy rival to the Yosemite.'
Per Prag, *Mountain Holidays in Norway*, 1963

THE DERBYSHIRE DALE OF WATER-CUM-JOLLY, lush and green during summer, was cold and white with hoar frost on the night before Christmas Eve 1964. The limestone crags glowed palely in the moonlight, and the river flowed slowly and noiselessly between ice-rimmed banks.

Inside our tent, it was warm and cosy. The pub was a long way, and huddling deeper into our sleeping bags John Amatt and I decided to do without a beer. We'd be having enough over Christmas. The Primus stove roared cheerily, melting the thick frost that had formed on the canvas during the day. We were content, sipping at a hot, sweet brew of tea and taking occasional bites of warm, rum-flavoured Christmas pudding. With a long and pleasant night ahead of us, the conversation dwelt on the forthcoming festivities, the day's climbing, last summer's climbs and where to go next year.

I had been trying to find out about Iceland for some time,

thinking of a trip there, but wasn't having much success with my enquiries. As the possibilities seemed slim, the subject reverted to Norway where John had been the previous summer and I had been in 1962. Both of us knew about the legendary Troll Wall, the last of the great north faces to remain unclimbed and the tallest and steepest rock wall in Europe. It was a great subject for discussion idling in the luxurious warmth of a tent in Derbyshire, but surely way out of our class.

Still, it was an exciting idea, and we talked into the early hours of the morning, becoming increasingly enthusiastic. We knew that the wall was the North Face of Trollryggen, which rises to a height of 5,750 feet. A north face always sounds very dramatic in the newspapers but unfortunately they hardly ever get any sunshine, which was a bit depressing, especially as the weather so far north is very variable, being only about three hundred miles south of the Arctic Circle. We preferred our climbs in the sun. We also knew the East Pillar of Trollryggen had recently been climbed by Ralph Hoibakk and Arne Randers Heen – the man who had climbed Reka four years before us, in 1958. Being well over 5,000 feet and with almost twice that amount of climbing, it was reputed to be the longest and most difficult route in Northern Europe, taking most parties at least two days, and many much longer. We thought if we ever decided to attempt the Troll Wall, this would be a good challenge to test our fitness. To the southwest, the peak presents only snow slopes, providing the normal means of ascent and descent. Beyond these few details, we knew almost nothing.

My passing glimpse of its lower half, gloomy and foreboding below the rain clouds, whilst hitching back from Lofoten in 1962 had revealed nothing, except that bad weather was a distinct possibility. The only people we knew personally who had seen it were two members of our club, Paul Seddon and Brian Hodgkinson, both good climbers with many first ascents to their credit. They had come home to England after climbing in Romsdal in 1963, where they had done the first British ascent of the East Face of Kongen, a 3,500-foot route with a three-sentence description. They had seen the Troll Wall both from the valley and from its upper edge and said it looked almost impossible. Descriptions in guidebooks and other reports – vague and half-remembered – suggested the wall was smooth and holdless for 5,000 feet and would require expansion bolts almost all the way.

This was highly improbable, we decided, and after Christmas got down to finding out a little more about the myth of the Troll Wall. We wrote urgently to everyone we knew who had been in the area. Colin Mortlock and Pete Emms furnished us with photos of the wall and at last we had some indication of what we were up against. It looked steep to be sure, and was quite possibly vertical throughout with more than its fair share of overhangs. But it was certainly neither smooth nor holdless. Furthermore, there seemed to be a number of huge corners in the lower half and something that looked very much like a gully in the upper section. This, we felt, could be the key to an ascent.

We wrote to Arne Randers Heen who lived at Åndalsnes only eight miles from the wall, and was possibly Norway's most famous mountaineer, at that time sixty years old, but still climbing and guiding. Arne had a string of first ascents to his name, going back to the 1930s, which included the first ascent of Trollryggen's East Pillar. He confirmed that a gully existed in the upper part of the wall. Nevertheless, he thought the ascent of the wall would be the hardest climb undertaken in Europe, needing artificial aid almost all the way.

We were still not convinced, and were keen to have a go that summer. After all, such a blatant challenge wasn't going to be left unclimbed forever and time was passing. Five other members of the Rimmon were equally sceptical and ready to form an expedition. We wrote hurriedly to potential sponsors. Jack Longland, President of the British Mountaineering Council, agreed to act as patron, giving us credibility, and the Bergen Line Shipping Company offered us a generous concession on the North Sea fare, making it possible to travel out for a reconnaissance.

Being, at the time, the only one out of work, I left in early March with another club member, Brian 'Smiler' Woods, who took a couple of weeks off work for the trip. We arrived in Åndalsnes, over two hundred miles north of Bergen, after a week of heavy snowfall. To the south, just visible above the fresh whiteness of nearer snow-capped peaks was the dark, jagged skyline of the wall. The summit spires, reminiscent of Chamonix aiguilles, were known to the locals as trolls – the mountain giants of Norwegian mythology.

According to legend, the trolls lived on Dovrefjell high above Romsdal and had been to a wedding at Trollkirka, a cave with a waterfall inside at Elnesvågen, near Molde. Returning late at night after a few too many beers, they were caught by the rising sun, which turned them to stone. So there they still stand, Trollgubben, Trollkkjerringa, Brura, Brudgommen and the Brurjentene: the old man and woman, their faces looking out over the wall, their daughter, the bride, with her bridegroom and the bridesmaids following behind. Below them, hidden from view, was their last stronghold – Trollveggen, the Wall of the Trolls.

We got our first view of it the following morning, picking our way cautiously over the frozen river Rauma with the blue-shadowed verticality of the wall less than two miles away. It was definitely big, but not 5,000 feet, that was certain. Numerous snow patches proved without doubt that despite reports to the contrary, there were ledges on the wall. As we struggled heavily laden through the soft, knee-deep powder, our eyes kept straying upwards, scanning the wall's shadowed contours for possible lines of weakness.

Once in the birch woods, we trampled out a hollow almost two feet deep in the powder snow and pitched the tent. The temperature was way below zero so we had a warm meal before preparing our gear for a closer look at the wall in the morning. The snow-flecked trolls glittered in the late afternoon sun as their shadows lengthened across the valley, creeping up in icy fingers towards the towering, shining summit of the Romsdalshorn in the east. The muffled roar of distant avalanches was the only sound that broke the winter stillness when, deep in our duvets and sleeping bags, we curled up for the night, wondering what we would discover the next day.

We woke early, breath misting in the cold air of the tent and, without leaving the warmth of our sleeping bags, cooked an unhurried breakfast. Outside in the dry cold, the snow remained soft and powdery and avalanches were once again starting to fall from the high peaks as the sun caught the summits. Our boots, despite being with us in the tent, were stiff and frozen as we stepped out into the crisp freshness of the morning and filled the sacks with essential gear, fingers sticking to the cold metal of carabiners and ice-axes.

Then we set off, ploughing our way through the deep snow and struggling through the tangled birch trees, which constantly showered us with icy crystals of snow knocked from their branches. Snow lay everywhere, concealing gaps between huge boulders down which both of us disappeared at frequent intervals, gasping as the fine powder found its way down our sleeves and collars, much to each other's amusement. It was consequently some time before we emerged from the woods at the base of the long slope that leads steeply up to the foot of the wall. Wading upwards, it was obvious that the top of the slope would be the only vantage point we could reach. The dangerous condition of the snow meant it would be inadvisable, if not completely impossible, to reach the summits opposite the face to photograph it as we'd planned. Fortunately this proved unnecessary.

After four hours of exhausting work, each alternately forcing a path through the snow, now almost waist deep, we finally arrived at a point level with the foot of the wall and on the opposite side of the huge amphitheatre from which it rises. With the naked eye it was possible to discern two very obvious weaknesses up the face. Looking through binoculars, both appeared feasible, but despite the snow ledges seen previously, they looked alarmingly steep. Indeed, most of the remainder of the wall almost lived up to its reputation of being smooth and overhanging. It was clear we would have to concentrate on these two possibilities.

The left-hand route followed a line of snow ledges and a huge dièdre, which led to a groove on the north east arête. Unfortunately, this groove, although on the very edge of the wall, was actually part of the East Pillar and thus avoided our objective, the Troll Wall. It was a case of Hobson's choice. There seemed to be just one remaining possibility. This seemed to follow what we hoped would be a series of slabs trending leftwards up the wall and at right angles to the general plane of the face. Because of its situation, we were unable to see the details of it, other than the profile, but snow ledges indicated a possible bivouac place near the bottom, and a large hanging snow basin in the centre of the wall, which was the next obvious objective. Between these was the steepest slab, which we named the Great Slab, and above the Central Basin a second slab – the Narrow Slab – appeared to lead up into the summit gully we had spotted on photos.

This was the only natural line on the wall we could see. We estimated its vertical height to be about 3,000 feet though the actual climb would obviously be much longer. We were also convinced it could be climbed without the use of too much artificial aid. The other route, up the North Wall and the East Pillar looked to offer more choice of line, but starting from a point lower down the slope we thought it would be in the region of 4,000 feet in vertical height. We decided to regard it as our alternative choice, should the other route prove impossible. After taking photos of the wall, and sketching both routes, noting all relevant features, we descended, stumbling down the tedious snow slopes before struggling back through the birch woods to the camp. We had seen enough to know the climb was possible.

For three days we waited, hoping the snow would solidify and allow further exploration, but the temperature remained below freezing and the snow stayed powdery and deep. Satisfied we had achieved our aim and could do no more, we finally left for Åndalsnes by the frozen river and ice-covered road. The coastal steamer carried us south to Bergen calling at isolated villages whose brightly painted houses formed a patchwork of colour against the snowy background. From Bergen, we returned to England across the dark heaving swell of the wintry North Sea. Now we could estimate the type and quantity of equipment required, and start to plan the trip in earnest.

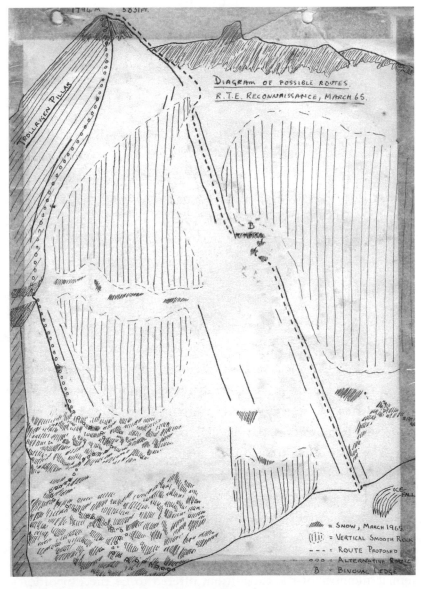

The reconnaissance team's first sketch of the Troll Wall.

Four

Preparations

Expedition Aid Plea Refused
Sympathy but not a penny from the Council
'Councillor Jim Whitehead commented, "if these people can go on these long expeditions to far off places, it seems unfair to apply to the local authority for assistance." Councillor Roger Tanner said in our support that he regretted the fact that a stage had been reached in this country where a lot more was spent on people going wrong than on those wanting to go right.'
Oldham Chronicle

HAVING DECIDED A ROUTE WAS POSSIBLE, we now had to choose a team. John was in favour of asking some of Britain's top climbers, but I preferred to limit it to our club: the Rimmon Mountaineering Club. After all, there were already five other members very interested in joining us and the club had chipped in to help cover our fare. If an expedition can be formed amongst friends, that's so much the better. They know each other's idiosyncrasies and, allowing for them, can better enjoy their company. Furthermore, all of us wanted to do the climb not only for ourselves as a personal challenge, but also on behalf of the club. We shared a common aim.

Margaret Woodcock, a good climber who became the only female member of the expedition, offered to be the expedition's cook and camp organiser. I had already been on an expedition with its own cook and knew how everyone had appreciated returning from a climb to find a good warm meal ready waiting. So I was more than happy with her offer, especially as she was my girlfriend. And given the lads who were on the expedition, it would be useful to have Maggie around to stop us sinking into typical male squalor.

Other than myself, none of the lads were above the age of twenty or had any great experience of long, sustained routes. Only Bill Tweedale had done any climbing outside England and Wales, and this on the smaller Dolomite faces. Nevertheless, he, Tony 'Nick' Nicholls and Rob Holt had done numerous Extremely Severe climbs in the Lake District, North Wales and on the gritstone and limestone cliffs of the Peak District and Yorkshire, some of them first ascents. Their technical capabilities were

Margaret Woodcock at Base Camp. *Photo: Margaret Woodcock*

beyond doubt. Beyond that, they were good company and reliable. Nick was a bit of an unsung hero, having done the second ascent and first on-sight lead of the infamous *Wall of Horrors* at Almscliff. It was typical of Nick, both in how he climbed it and the fact that such a momentous event should escape attention. Many people still think it was the Leeds University climber John Syrett who did the second ascent several years later. Nick had been climbing at Almscliff with a friend when some of the local lads, seeing he looked pretty handy on the grit, pointed it out to him. He knew it had a bit of a reputation but typically for Nick he went at it like a bull at a gate, thinking if he fell off he could just roll when he hit the deck.

John Amatt also had limited experience of big routes, though he had two or three previously unclimbed faces to his credit, some of up to 3,000 feet. These he had climbed the previous year in

Left to right, back row – Tony Howard, Rob Holt, Bill Tweedale, Tony 'Nick' Nicholls, John Amatt. Front row – Jeff Heath, Margaret Woodcock. *Photo: Daily Express*

Norway but none had taken more than a day. Jeff Heath on the other hand had done very little climbing whatsoever and it was less than a year since he had joined the club as a complete novice. However, all the climbers had one factor in common. We were all convinced that working as a team we could climb the wall, and keep it as a club ascent. We had with us some of the finest climbers in the club and with the correct equipment and enough time the route would surely be 'in the bag'.

The problem of time off work was soon solved. Everyone agreed to give in their notice for the end of June. The whole summer was ours. The next problem was acquiring sufficient food, clothing and equipment. We could never hope to raise enough money to purchase all our requirements. With only twelve weeks to go before we planned to sail for Norway, we had some hard work ahead of us if we were going to leave properly supplied.

During the first two weeks following the reconnaissance, we worked out the basic details of the expedition, which we called, grandiosely, 'The 1965 Rimmon Trolltind Expedition'. Base Camp – another rather pretentious term – would obviously be situated as conveniently as possible between the wall and the road. There would also have to be an Advance Camp, which would be at the head of the steep scree slopes as near to the foot of the wall as possible. We hoped some snow would remain here in summer, otherwise all the water would have to be carried up from Base Camp, which was a dismal prospect.

The ascent of the wall itself proved a much more controversial subject. We finally agreed that if there was not too much artificial work the route could possibly be completed in six days. This would only be possible if the lower stages had been equipped with fixed rope to enable sufficient food and equipment to be taken onto the wall and left at convenient dumps. It was decided that all six male members should work on the fixed ropes, whilst John, Nick, Bill and I would form the final climbing team, Rob being the youngest member of the expedition and Jeff the least experienced.

The number of pegs we should take proved even more controversial. From the start we had decided to leave them all in place as was the practice in the Dolomites. This meant we would have to carry enough for the whole route. The only disadvantages we could think of were the expense, which would have to be resolved, and the sheer effort of carrying that number of pegs. At least the weight would decrease throughout the climb, so we weren't too concerned. Leaving the pegs in place would not only save a great deal of work and energy on the part of the second who normally has to remove them, but would also mean a considerable saving in time as well. If we had to retreat off the wall, perhaps in bad weather or to help an injured team member, leaving the pegs in would make it easier. More than anything else, we all felt that on such a major ascent all pegs should be left in place so that future climbers could benefit from our efforts.

Considering these factors, and the pessimism of everyone we contacted who had seen the wall, we finally decided on the following quantities:

150 assorted horizontal pitons
150 assorted channel pitons
30 assorted micro pitons
30 assorted wooden wedges
30 expansion bolts

The weight of all that ironmongery was horrifying. We also decided, in case of accidents, that each climber should have his own peg hammer and set of etriers and, as there would be three ropes of two on the lower wall, we would need at least a hundred of the new lightweight alloy carabiners. To help carry this equipment whilst climbing, we would use a new version of a safety belt I had designed for aid climbing in Derbyshire, to which the amount of gear required for each day could be attached. We also designed special bivouac sacks and, as the number of bivouac ledges was in doubt, special bivouac seats to hang like cradles from the wall.

So to our list of pegs, we now added a long and expensive list of essential food and equipment:

One month's provisions for Base Camp – mostly tinned

Two weeks' provisions for Advance Camp – mostly dehydrated

Two weeks' rations for the wall – mostly dehydrated and of high calorific value

100 carabiners

30 slings

2 short-shafted ice-axes in case of ice in the Summit Gully

6 piton hammers

3 hand drills

6 pairs etriers – metal or wooden runged, made by us

30 tape etriers – designed by us

6 harnesses – designed by us

3 300-foot climbing ropes

7 300-foot lightweight Ulstron, polypropylene ropes for fixing and sack-hauling

6 bivouac seats – designed by us

3 two-man bivouac sacks – designed by us

2 gas stoves

20 cylinders

6 duvet jackets, cagoules, helmets, and so on

Pans, water bottles, and so on

We already had much of the above, but even so the cost of the remainder including our return fares to and from Romsdal came to, what was to us, the startling figure of £750, or two months wages from each of us. Being on the dole, I got a job earning the princely sum of £15 a week working on the construction of Dovestones Reservoir in Chew Valley, almost £5 more than the local council paid for labourers.

We began writing anxiously to firms, many of which had helped previous expeditions. One night a week we'd meet to see if any of us had any news, but always the conversation would turn to the actual climbing of the wall. It was becoming our sole obsession. Eventually, with only six weeks to go, we had a list of over fifty firms who had generously offered to help us. Final details were sent to each and in the following weeks, Bill's parents' spare room began to fill slowly with an assortment of boxes and parcels. Each one was thankfully checked in, but our worries were far from over.

The most essential item, the climbing ropes, had not yet arrived and no word had arrived from the manufacturers. The fixed ropes hadn't turned up either and we hadn't yet managed to find a firm who could supply us with dehydrated vegetables. Furthermore, we could find no one who could supply us with the type of gloves we wanted and the newly designed belts, seats and bivouac tents were still being made. With less than a month before we left for Norway, our nerves were becoming shredded.

Another problem was money. Thanks to the generosity of our sponsors most of us now had just enough for the expedition. Others were not so lucky. Jeff, Rob and Nick were still scraping the barrel and working every moment they could get. Even so, for some reason no one could quite understand, Nick still didn't have enough cash for his boat fare. Finally, he raised enough for a deposit at the travel agent and we began to breathe more easily.

All of us were out climbing without fail every weekend and climbing as well as we ever had, though lacking any transport we were forced to concentrate on the gritstone and limestone cliffs of the local Peak District. On the former, Nick, Bill and Rob were ticking off some of the fiercest Extremes, whilst on the latter we were concentrating on the technical problems of artificial climbing.

Three days before we were due to sail Nick finally scraped together enough money to pay the balance for his fare and at last we were able to collect our tickets. Even so, there was still no news of the climbing ropes, and the safety helmets hadn't arrived yet either. We had to pack everything without them and hope that both would turn up before John, who had to leave a few days after us, finally departed.

The living room at Bill's was in chaos, as the ton of food and equipment was somehow packed into twenty-eight boxes, kit bags and rucksacks, carried outside and stored for departure. By the end of the day we were exhausted and the room was empty, but at least we were now ready to go. Even better, on the eve of our departure, the ropes finally arrived, seven three-hundred-foot lengths of beautiful new cord. We sighed with relief. Having packed them lovingly into our rucksacks, and with assurances that the helmets were definitely on their way, we could finally relax. So we went to the pub for a drink to celebrate.

FIVE

The Journey

Greenfield man to attempt 5,000ft rock face climb
'At his home this week, Tony Howard said, "Norway is magnificent climbing country. By making this assault on the Trolltind Wall we want to prove to British climbers the unique opportunities there."'
Oldham Chronicle

MONDAY 28TH JUNE. The thirty-seater coach we had hired specially for our journey to Newcastle Docks arrived promptly at 8.30 a.m. Half an hour later the equipment was loaded and we were off. John had another few days of work to do before he could travel out to join us. The rest of us settled back in our seats to enjoy the trip and dream about the wall. Sitting in the coach and travelling north, it was hard to believe that after five months of planning we were actually on our way. In a matter of days we would be in Romsdal and at the foot of the wall. Everyone had finished with the routine of work for at least two months. We were heading for the unknown. I was full of that feeling of elation I always have on such occasions.

The radio belted out songs as the coach hummed northwards. The Supremes, The Stones and Donovan were in the charts. The Beatles were at number one with their Ticket to Ride –

and so were we. After stopping at a transport café for a brew, we set off again through the busy streets of Newcastle and down to the docks. Once aboard ship I would really believe we were on our way. We stood watching the crate with all our gear standing idly on the dockside. The hold was filling rapidly and nobody was going near our precious cargo. I was just starting to get anxious, when it was hooked up to a crane and swung aboard. Now surely, nothing could go wrong. We wandered off in search of the bar and broke into the first of our valuable funds.

The journey across to Oslo was pleasant and the weather good though cool. Out on deck, I leaned over the rail to watch the sun go down, the ocean turning to gold as it slipped below the horizon. Someone unused to sailing standing on an upper deck above me chose this moment to be violently sick on my head, which gave everyone a laugh. I spent the rest of the evening in the showers trying to get rid of the smell.

Arriving in Oslo the following morning we were met by a lorry that ferried our equipment to the station. Our train wasn't due to leave till six o'clock that evening, so we had a full day at our disposal to view Norway's capital. With no particular itinerary in mind we strolled across the city and sauntered through the grounds of the Royal Palace. Then someone had the idea of visiting the Kon-Tiki Museum. After five increasingly hectic months, it was a relief not to be doing much. Five minutes later, however, we were in a state of shock.

Wandering past a newsagent's displaying that day's papers, Nick suddenly said with astonishment, 'Hey! Look at that. It's a photo of the wall.' Sure enough, there it was, right in the centre of the front page and, worst of all, a route was marked up it with a bold white line. Had someone beaten us to it? What a fiasco that would be after all our planning and painstaking preparations. Mustering my small knowledge of Norwegian I managed a rough translation of the inch-high headline:

'NORWEGIAN CLIMBERS CHALLENGE BRITISH TO ASCENT OF TROLLVEGGEN. NORWAY'S HONOUR AT STAKE.'

Lower down, it continued:

'THE RACE IS ON.'

Who were the British? We hadn't heard of any other climbers going out to attempt the wall. I skimmed hurriedly through the article, unable to translate its contents, but then there it was in black and white, unmistakable amongst the Norwegian print: the Rimmon Mountaineering Club. They were talking about us. How, I wondered, did the Norwegians know we were coming out?

This news completely demoralised us. We sat down on the pavement, our carefree world completely destroyed, and cursed the Norwegian climbers. Whoever heard of climbers openly challenging another team to the ascent of a wall or summit? This sounded like the race between Scott and Amundsen. Surely they must realise what a great deal of hard work we had already put into the expedition? We decided it was either an extremely dirty trick or there must be some mistake.

Climbing is not generally considered a competitive sport but, of course, everyone with ambition wants to do well. As in every era, the amount of equipment used was of fundamental importance. Simply 'nailing' our way to the summit to grab a quick first ascent was not our bag. Treating the ascent of any rock wall, whatever its size, as an actual race would be almost universally frowned on, so we had no intention of changing our plans. We were going to do the route in the best style possible, however long it took.

Perhaps we were naive, but we couldn't imagine any climber, whatever his attitude, getting involved in some kind of contest. Come what may, we wouldn't be drawn in. Scanning through the article again, we searched for the Norwegian names and finally spotted them: Arne Naess, Arne Oppdal and Ralph Hoibakk. All three, we knew, were famous Norwegian mountaineers. Surely they would never do such a thing as the paper suggested and announce it to the world as a challenge?

It wasn't until we'd calmed down and thought objectively about the situation over a meal, that the most disastrous implication of the situation finally occurred to us. As far as we knew there was only one possible route that followed the wall completely, and this we considered to be 'our' route. If the Norwegians were in fact already there, then they must almost certainly be on that route.

This thought was, if anything, more awful than if they had already completed the ascent. All we could do would be to sit at the bottom of the face and watch them climb the route on which we had spent so much time and effort choosing and planning. The realisation started us cursing again and every Norwegian climber who had ever breathed the word 'Trollveggen' should have been quaking in his boots.

The only thing we could do was to catch the earliest possible train up to Romsdal and find out just what was happening. We walked back to the station full of ill-tempered oaths, only to find that the train we had tickets for was, in fact, the earliest anyway. Feeling absolutely frustrated we sat down in a dismal mood for the long wait. We couldn't even muster up enough spirit to carry out our original intention of visiting the Kon-Tiki Museum. Instead, we played cards and looked continually at our watches, wishing it was already six o'clock.

At a quarter to six, a train pulled into the platform and we loaded our gear into the luggage van before going to look for our seats. Strangely, the coaches didn't seem to have the right numbers, but we finally managed to ask a porter in broken Norwegian if this was in fact the train for Romsdal and Åndalsnes.

'No,' he replied, 'This is going to Trondheim. The Åndalsnes train will be here at six o'clock.' By this time, doors were shutting and the train was obviously preparing to leave. Our gear, of course, was still in the luggage van. We dashed down the platform hoping we had enough time to throw everything out, but the door was locked. It seemed everything was against us.

We grabbed the astonished porter and tried to make him understand: 'Our equipment is in there for Romsdal. It's on the wrong train!'

All he could do was smile idiotically and reply, 'Romsdal, ja, ja, okay.' Then I saw why. Though the train we'd left was moving, the luggage van was staying put. It had been brought in by the Trondheim train, then uncoupled and left for our train to collect. It was us who were the idiots.

Just before six, our train finally arrived, and making doubly sure this was, in fact, the correct one, we began to load our personal gear into the carriage. At that moment a friendly looking Norwegian lad came up and asked if we were the English climbers going to Trollveggen. We said, yes, we were, and thought, warily, 'How the hell do you know?'

He said his name was Ole Enersen and that he had seen our equipment and, as he would soon be joining his friends who were also climbing in Romsdal, he thought he would like to meet us. This turned out later to have been the understatement of the year. We asked if he knew anything about the newspaper story and he told us that to the best of his knowledge some of the Norwegian climbers mentioned in the article wouldn't be finishing work for some weeks yet, whilst the others certainly had no plans to attempt the wall this year and, most reassuringly of all, it hadn't been climbed.

According to Ole, the whole story was nothing but a piece of badly informed journalistic fantasy and, as far as he knew, none of the three climbers mentioned knew anything about it. We declared the story the champion hoax of 1965 and we started to enjoy ourselves again. As the train pulled slowly out of the station we thanked Ole for his news and said we hoped to see him and his friends in Romsdal. He smiled a little at this remark, and no wonder, because, as we were soon to discover, Ole was a member of the Norwegian team that really was already on their way to attempt the wall.

The three-hundred mile journey northwards to Romsdal was to take twelve hours overnight, so feeling happier than we had all day, we settled down to rest and enjoy the countryside despite the weather, which was deteriorating slowly as we travelled up long, green pastoral valleys, over narrow bridges across thundering torrents and ever deeper into the thickly wooded hills. By the first light of morning, we were crossing the misty snow-clad heights above Dombas where the waters of the Rauma gather in small, clear streams before cascading in mighty waterfalls down into the dark green depths of the Romsdal valley 2,000 feet below.

So steeply do the sides of the valley plunge downwards that the train has to descend in immense zigzags, once actually tunneling into the hillside in a great descending spiral before emerging directly below its own tracks. The mists were clinging tenaciously to the pine and birch trees of the forests and a thin rain was smearing the glass of the compartment windows when we finally reached the valley bottom.

We looked in vain for the towering bastions of the wall, but could see only the damp, grey screes disappearing into the mist as they had when I had visited Romsdal three years ago. Disappointed, we began searching for our anoraks and duvets as the small station of Romsdalshorn could only be a few minutes down the line. At least the bad weather would probably mean no other climbers would be on the wall. And that might give us a chance to stake a claim on our route. Despite what Ole had told us, we couldn't quite get the newspaper story out of our minds and we wanted to make sure we could keep to our planned route. This was our only real worry.

As the train arrived at the platform, I jumped from the carriage and the lads started to pass the equipment out to me. They had hardly begun when the train set off again. I was left standing foolishly alone with a couple of rucksacks while the others stared out of the carriage door in astonishment. All we could do was laugh and wave goodbye to each other. Fortunately, someone must have realised something was wrong because the train stopped again a hundred yards down the track and we were able to resume unloading our gear, this time into someone's field. Was anything ever going to go right?

With the ton of gear off the train, our next problem was transporting it to Fiva Farm, which we knew was within a mile of a decent campsite. We explained our predicament to the stationmaster and after a couple of phone calls he returned to tell us a lorry would be along in ten minutes. This time, nothing went wrong and for a reasonable charge he took the equipment and us to the farm. It was now only a matter of carrying everything up in relays along a path through the birch woods to an idyllic campsite by the river's edge.

By mid-afternoon we had erected the two large tents, arranged all the boxes and bags of food and equipment neatly inside and unpacked the cooking equipment and sleeping bags. A fire was lit and we were just about to relax in true macho-style to watch Margaret cook a meal and make a brew, when the farmer arrived. 'Very sorry,' he said, 'you can't camp near the river. It's one of the best salmon rivers in Norway and you'll disturb the fish.'

This was just about the last straw, but since we should have checked first, it was our fault and nothing could be done about it. We re-packed everything. Down came the tents amidst much futile cursing and we dragged the whole lot a hundred yards back to a small clearing in the trees. This, according to the farmer, would be alright, so we re-erected the tents, replaced the equipment inside, lit another fire and lay down exhausted. Surely nothing else could go wrong now?

Margaret cooked a marvellous meal and we lay in our sleeping bags with a first-class brew, replete, tired and content. We were here at last and, of competitive Norwegian climbers, there was neither sight nor sound. The only noise was the distant river and the rain, which dripped quietly on the canvas and hissed among the embers of the fire.

PART THREE

Assault
Preparations

Six

Advance Camp

The 'Magnificent 7' aim to beat 4,000ft rock face

Their skill will be pitted against the smoothly vertical and often overhanging North Wall of Trolltind in Romsdal, Norway, described as "one of the longest rock faces of its kind in the world, a masterpiece of mountain architecture and one of the most difficult climbing problems left in Europe."'

Tom Waghorn, *Manchester Evening News*

IT WAS LATE, ALMOST MID-DAY, when we woke the following morning for our first day in Romsdal. The weather was still poor, with the whole of the wall concealed by mist. As we were finishing our breakfast a reporter from the local press arrived wanting a story. Our arrival was already common knowledge. We asked if there were in fact any Norwegians attempting the wall. 'Oh yes,' he replied with obvious pride.

On further questioning it emerged that these climbers had nothing whatsoever to do with the fictional newspaper story, which, he said, had been as much a surprise for them as it had been for us. They too were equally annoyed by its implications. But whoever these unknown climbers were, the problem of which route they were following remained worryingly unsolved.

The reporter said, as far as he knew, the Norwegians hadn't started yet, but were camped on the screes at the foot of the wall. There was still a chance we could claim our route. We thanked him profusely and began to pack the climbing equipment and a tent for Advance Camp. If we could just get up there and fix a rope on the first pitch of our route to stake our claim, then we could take it easy.

By four in the afternoon, all the essential gear was crammed into five packs weighing sixty pounds each. A light drizzle was falling, but eager to get started we left Mag to prepare a meal for our return and set off into the birch woods. By the time we emerged at the foot of the scree slope we were drenched by the rain knocked from the trees as our ungainly packs snagged on the low branches.

The flanks of the scree leading into the amphitheatre below and opposite the wall were still buried in snow and we heard frequent avalanches falling from the summit gullies of Store Trolltind, directly above us in the mist. We couldn't be certain where they were landing but as these lower slopes seemed untouched and safe we followed them up leftwards in a long diagonal climb for half a mile onto the screes.

By now, although the rain was falling steadily, the mist was beginning to lift and we could see the avalanches pouring down above us, to our right. The mist was also clearing from Trollveggen on our left and we craned our heads in astonishment as the summit spires – those infamous trolls – appeared high above, wreathed by the swirling clouds. I was the only one who had seen the wall before and knew what to expect.

We scanned the wall carefully with binoculars and agreed the chosen route seemed the only feasible one. More importantly, we could see no climbers or fixed ropes on it – or anywhere else for that matter. On the other hand, the amount of snow still present was shocking and small avalanches were continually belching out of the Summit Gully. We watched in amazement as what must have been large masses of snow appeared to drift slowly down the wall, never touching the rock. They finally dissipated into smaller pieces, spinning and drifting in space and landing many seconds later with muffled thuds on the snow slopes beneath and over fifty feet out from the base of the wall. Any climbing would obviously be out of the question in these conditions. We could only hope the rain would do its work and remove the snow.

Deeply impressed, we continued up the screes feeling horribly unfit under the weight of our loads. When we finally reached the snowline at the head of the amphitheatre, there were no ledges or sheltered places anywhere. If we were to camp here, we would have to dig a platform out of the screes to give us a level area and some protection from possible falling stones. The larger boulders were easily pushed out of the way and a rough ledge soon manufactured using our ice-axes. It was just large enough to erect the mountain tent with the guy-lines held down by boulders dangling over the edge.

Yet it didn't give us much shelter and looked rather precarious. We were also worried about avalanches as the large ones from Store Trolltind were still falling frequently only a couple of hundred yards away behind us. As the snow slopes above the tent looked safe and showed no marks of falling stones, we finally decided the tent was in as safe a position as possible and piled all the climbing equipment and provisions inside before preparing to leave.

It was then we spotted the Norwegian tent far below on the screes under the lower end of wall. We shouted down, but could see no movement. There was nothing to be done, so leaving our tent and its precious contents to the mercy of the trolls we set off down the screes towards Base Camp, barely visible in the trees below.

By the time we got there we were soaked to the skin, after battling our way once more through the undergrowth, only to find John had arrived with our crash-hats and was sitting inside the tent, clean, dry and smiling. Mag had seen us coming back down the screes and a hot meal was waiting. Between mouthfuls we told John about the last few days' events. It was early morning before we finally settled down and the skies were still light with the glow of the midnight sun.

When we woke it was noon and we stayed in bed for breakfast. The weather was still vile so we decided to have an easy day. But in the middle of the afternoon we heard voices outside, and looking out saw Ole and three other climbers. In his old and well-worn climbing clothes he looked a different person to the suave young man we had met in Oslo. The others, all with large bulging rucksacks and well-patched trousers, looked equally 'hard'. Then we guessed. These were the four mysterious Norwegian climbers whose tent we had seen below the wall!

Ole introduced us to the other three, Leif Norman Patterson, Jon Teigland and Odd Eliassen, all names we had heard, or seen in *Alpinismus* magazine. Two had been to the Himalaya. They were quite a team. We exchanged greetings cautiously until we discovered that they too wanted nothing of the publicity given to the proposed Norwegian ascent by the press. Like us, it seemed they had been planning to climb the wall for some time, and that we should both arrive together was an unfortunate coincidence. Or at least, that's what they said, but we still wondered if Arne Randers Heen, who we had been writing to since the previous winter, had put the word out amongst Norwegian climbers in the hope they would climb the wall before someone from abroad did – and if so, who could blame him?

Putting our doubts to one side, we asked them in for a brew and a meal and commiserated with each other on the dreadful weather. The conversation wavered tentatively around the question of choice of routes. Apart from a few vague indications, no one would really commit themselves and the topic was left well alone with no hard feelings on either side. We did get the impression, however, that their choice was different from ours and the subject changed agreeably enough to climbing in Europe and elsewhere. Both parties were glad to have met and to be on easy terms when they finally left for their camp. If only they were trying a different route, then everything would work out okay. We weren't bothered who reached the top first. It might be important for the Norwegians, if they were concerned about national honour, but it was irrelevant to us. What mattered was getting on our chosen route. Everything seemed to be turning out fine after all, except the weather.

All next day it continued to rain but, hoping for the best, the six of us waved goodbye to Mag in the late afternoon and set off again for Advance with another thirty pounds of food and gear each. With the smaller loads we reached the tent in just over two hours, almost halving our previous time. Now armed with a shovel borrowed from the farmer, we dug out another platform for a second tent and, as John, Bill, Nick and myself were to stay up for the night in case the weather improved, Rob and Jeff finally departed leaving us alone in the damp, grey mist.

Inside the mountain tent, which had been pitched previously, everything was in chaos. Equipment had been tossed in almost to the roof and it took Nick and I a quarter of an hour before we'd managed to clear enough room for one of us to crawl inside.

The team at Advance Camp, from left to right – Bill Tweedale, John Amatt, Tony 'Nick' Nicholls, Jeff Heath, Rob Holt and Tony Howard. *Photo: Margaret Woodcock*

It was another quarter of an hour before we had all the equipment outside and stowed in the bivouac sacks. Then at last, we were able to take off our wet clothes and get into our sleeping bags. With the stove on, the tent was soon warm and before long we were tucking into a hot stew.

In the shadow of the amphitheatre, enclosed by the high walls of Trollryggen and Store Trolltind, and with the double thickness of the tent and flysheet, it was soon dark in the tent despite the half-light still illuminating the valley below. Settling down, we could hear the avalanches that were still falling and had been half forgotten in the activity of the evening. In the stillness of the high corrie they seemed fearfully loud and close as they thundered down from the walls above to land with a roar on the screes. But as long as they continued to fall in the same place we were out of harm's way and accepted the sudden interruptions as part of the game.

What I did not reckon with, however, was the horrific crunching and crashing that woke me in the early morning and was getting closer all the time. In fact, it seemed to be bearing straight towards the tent. In a panic I struggled with the cords of the sleeve entrance and just managed to get my head outside as a boulder as large as the tent careered past only a few yards away. I looked at Nick. He was still peacefully asleep and blissfully unaware that a ton of instant death had narrowly missed the tent with us inside. Needless to say, there was no more sleep for me and as soon as I dared I woke Nick and we busied ourselves cooking breakfast. I told Nick the tale, but as far as he was concerned we were still in one piece. What was the point of worrying about it?

When John and Bill appeared from the other tent, John was more sympathetic as he too had seen the gigantic boulder. Like me he had spent the early hours of the morning wondering if the next one to fall would score a direct hit. We blamed it on the trolls and Bill laughingly suggested that the screes must be their bowling alley and our tents were the skittles. The stonefall was in reality caused by the incessant rain, which even now was still falling, causing the snowfields above the tents to loosen their icy grip on unseen rocks and boulders.

Following breakfast, we began to sort out the equipment. The weather was still hopeless but we could just see the bottom of the wall. With luck we would at least be able to find the start of our route and fix a rope up it. Just as we set off, the Norwegians appeared, toiling up the screes. Now we would definitely find out one way or another which route they intended doing. We shouted over to them, and they came across full of smiles. 'Awful weather isn't it,' said Leif, 'We started our climb yesterday, but didn't make much progress.'

So despite the weather they had begun. A canny lot, these Norwegians. We wondered where, and looked anxiously across to the wall for any sign of fixed ropes, hoping it wasn't 'our' route they had chosen but Leif pointed across to the centre of the most impossible looking part of the face and there, through binoculars, we could just make out their first hundred feet of fixed rope. They had started on the very lip of a huge overhang, above which, on close inspection, a superb crackline was visible straight up one of the smoothest and most vertical sections of the face. We viewed it with respect and admiration. It was a bold choice. Our climb, which as far as we were concerned followed the only natural weakness of the wall, was well to the right and seemed puny by comparison.

We showed them the route we had chosen, and Leif said they had considered it but thought there was too much danger from avalanches. The route they had decided on, although obviously much harder, overhung to such an extent that once on the wall, the danger of avalanches was non-existent. He hoped we too had considered the avalanche risk and we assured him we had and that until the snow cleared from the wall we would do little other than fix the ropes on the lower section. Now each party could go ahead without treading on the others' toes. Our friendship was finally sealed.

SEVEN

First Acquaintance

Mountain wall – two teams ready

'A British expedition which will try to be the first to conquer a 3,300-foot "unclimbable mountain wall" in the Romsdal valley... has arrived at the foot to find a Norwegian group already camped there says Reuters... They hope to climb the Troll Wall – an almost vertical polished wall with few fissures for footholds. Many experts say they doubt whether anyone will ever manage to climb the wall unless there is exceptionally good weather.'

Western Evening Herald, Plymouth

AFTER CHATTING WITH THE NORWEGIANS for a while, we finally left Advance armed with ice-axes, a small amount of climbing gear and a couple of fixed ropes. The snow above was not too soft despite the rain and we made reasonable progress as it steepened to meet the Introductory Wall where our climb would start.

The whole base of the crag bulged considerably. It was obvious our line of approach would have to be from the right where a ramp of slabs led into the centre of the crag. We were relieved to see that its upper lip also overhung for most of its length, confirming our hopes that, like the Norwegians, we would be protected from avalanches, at least during this early stage.

Tony Howard climbing the lower slabs of the Introductory Wall, on the fixed ropes. *Photo: John Amatt*

The last two hundred feet of snow led up very steeply to the edge of the bergschrund, below which a large mass of collapsed snow formed a bridge onto the slabs. We roped up and fixed a belay before I stepped out gingerly onto the snow bridge, but it seemed safe enough and another couple of strides brought me onto the rock. The climb had begun.

Immediately opposite was a natural hole in the rock through which we could fasten the fixed rope. It was an auspicious start. I led off happily across the slabs, now completely oblivious to the rain and glad to be climbing at last. Two hundred feet out I reached a good platform and behind, ideally situated, was a perfect spike for attaching the other end of the fixed rope. This was really great. The others joined me, equally wet but equally glad to have started so I led off again up a dripping groove to a smaller ledge some fifty feet above. The next obstacle, a small ten-foot wall, proved frustrating and after a couple of hopeless attempts I put a couple of belay pegs in and brought the others up to see what they could do.

The only chance of a free ascent was on the left side of the wall where a series of minute slime-covered balance holds led to a small ledge above. On dry gritstone and wearing rock shoes, it might just have been possible. Even so, Nick, who will always try anything, decided to have a go. Even in boots and waterlogged clothing he made surprisingly good progress and with sudden hope that somehow he might succeed I offered him my shoulder as a foothold. He trampled on me with complete disregard for the next five minutes, but despite all his efforts the ledge remained annoyingly out of reach.

This was ridiculous. Here we were on a small, four hundred foot crag, a mere appetizer before the main course of the wall, and we couldn't get up the first little obstacle that presented itself. We stood in the rain and thought. There was only one other way of overcoming the problem, and that was with pegs, and the only peg crack was directly under a waterfall on the right-hand edge of the wall. Everyone viewed it with distaste until John, obviously feeling in a heroic mood, decided he would literally take the plunge. We gladly gave him the necessary equipment and he stepped into the deluge trying to get the first peg in as quickly as possible, to pull up under a small overhang before he was drowned.

Gasping in the cold water, he finally moved up in his etriers and gained some respite from its incessant battering. The next peg went in rather too easily and came out again as he tested it. Another, a little higher, seemed better and he moved up again. Two more pegs and he was on the stance, thoroughly soaked but victorious. On the ledge below, we were not much drier and, having stood idly in the rain for some time, we were, like John, beginning to feel the cold.

We looked across to see how the Norwegians were faring and they seemed to be on their way down with another hundred feet of rope in place. Considering the conditions and the angle of their climb, that was good going. We decided to follow suit as soon as possible. Meanwhile, John continued up to the next decent ledge and Nick followed valiantly through the waterfall, taking the second fixed rope up and hanging a chain of tape etriers down the centre of the wall. With these in place its future ascent would present no problems so the day hadn't been wasted. The fixed rope was attached to the highest point and John and Nick returned down it to our ledge. We had established our claim.

With a sliding carabiner clipped from our waist belts to the fixed rope across the traverse, it was only a matter of moments to run across in tension and regain the snow slopes. A long, enjoyable glissade followed and by five o'clock we were back in Advance. Four hundred feet of fixed ropes were in position and the first obstacle had been passed, but as the weather seemed like staying bad for some time, we decided to return to Base. If the conditions remained unchanged, it would be impossible to go much higher in safety, but a couple of fine days might give the route a chance to dry out and reduce some of the avalanche danger.

The chief obstacle in this initial stage would be passing the snowfield poised on the upper edge of the Introductory Wall. Not only did it seem in danger of avalanching but, until we reached the crevice that undercut the whole length of the vertical wall above, we would also be exposed to danger from stonefall. The avalanche danger we could do little about except keep off the snow as much as possible and hope it would become safer with better weather. But we could reduce the risk of being hit by stonefall by making the most direct approach possible to the foot of the wall. Once there, we would be able to traverse below its overhanging base in safety, keeping between the rock and the snow until we reached the point where we must move onto the wall proper. This seemed to be about level with the upper edge of the snowfield. Above it, not far up the main wall, we could see what looked like a shallow cave. Perhaps this could be the First Bivouac?

The main danger in this part of the climb lay between the moment we left the top of the Introductory Wall and when we arrived at the foot of the main wall. From our position on the screes below Advance, we could see that this portion of the climb was made up of three sections. The first was up a long pitch of easy-angled rock.

Tony, Bill, John and Nick at the first bivouac on the first attempt. *Photo: Tony Howard*

Above this was the bottom edge of the snowfield. The next section would be over part of the snowfield that had already broken away from the main mass. This would bring us to the final section, across slabs between the overhanging snow wall at the foot of the main snowfield, and the large seracs that had detached themselves from it. Not a very inviting prospect, but if we could fasten the fixed ropes securely we would feel a bit happier.

When we arrived back at Base, there was no one around. We soon realised that not expecting us back for a couple of days, Mag, Rob and Jeff must have gone down to Åndalsnes for the evening. This was disappointing. We had been looking forward to Mag's cooking. But Bill rose to the occasion and by the time the others returned we were just finishing off a large and appetising stew.

That evening, we discussed how things were progressing and worked out a rota so there would always be four of us at Advance Camp to take advantage of any good weather. Although we were starting to doubt we would ever have any. The mist and rain had now persisted for five days and we had only managed to catch a fleeting glimpse of the whole of the wall on two occasions.

Next day, the miracle happened and we woke to the strange and novel experience of brilliant sunshine penetrating the chinks of the door flap and casting a beam of light onto the groundsheet. Outside, the canvas of the tents and even the trees and grass were steaming in the heat. And there, in all its splendour, was the Troll Wall.

Everyone staggered out half undressed, rubbing sleep from their eyes to gaze upwards at its stark blue-grey verticality. The rain had obviously been falling as snow on the summit, which was flecked in dazzling whiteness. After the last five days of dark swirling mists the whole panorama was breathtakingly magnificent in this sudden revelation. It seemed almost sacrilege to ignore it whilst we carried out the drab necessity of hanging up sodden clothes to dry.

We breakfasted outside, basking in the heat of the unbelievable sunshine. Wood was gathered for the fire, boots were cleaned, the food and equipment was checked. Even the tents were cleaned out and, finally, succumbing to Margaret's demands, all the pans and dishes were washed. The whole time, the sun beat down and the clothes dried with amazing speed.

Up above, the summit snows were disappearing and everywhere the gullies were spewing avalanches. The wall, which had always been black and water-covered, was drying at an astonishing rate and now looked rough, grey and inviting. Nearer camp, the huge slabs forming the lower half of the 5,000 foot East Face of Store Trolltind had been nothing but a vast sheet of running water since we arrived. Today, however, they had dried completely.

Rob and I couldn't resist the temptation of warm, dry rock, and wearing only shorts and lightweight rockboots we spent an enjoyable couple of hours on this king-sized version of Snowdonia's Idwal Slabs. The surface of the rock was covered in minute pebbles that had been washed down by the rain and melting snow. It was like climbing up ball-bearings on a smooth 45-degree slope. We ended in a small forest two hundred feet up and descended in a hilarious glissade, the ice-cold crystals of snow showering our bare, sun-warmed bodies.

Bill and Nick, on the other hand, had apparently not had enough water to satisfy them so they went for a swim in the roaring glacial waters of the river. They soon returned, refreshed and invigorated, but no amount of coaxing on their part could persuade us it was worthwhile. Later on, the Norwegians arrived with a couple of girlfriends who were helping them at camp. They too were having an easy day so we were able to discuss each other's progress as we munched on sandwiches.

They had been down for provisions and hoped to resume their climb tomorrow. Because of the large amount of aid-climbing necessary on their route, they expected to take at least four weeks on the ascent. Our route, we felt sure, we could complete in a fortnight if the weather held but no one was really bothered how long it took. If the weather stayed like this, we had all the time in the world. We were all looking forward to getting back on the wall. The fantasy of a 'race', conceived and promoted by the press, was laughable.

EIGHT

The Fixed Ropes

Local Team Faces Challenge
'A scramble to conquer Europe's most inaccessible mountain wall appeared today to be starting between Norwegian climbers and members of the Rimmon Mountaineering Club... a Norwegian expert said that if the two groups made simultaneous attempts to reach the top their ropes might be interwoven and cause difficulties...'
Oldham Chronicle

THE FOLLOWING MORNING WAS EQUALLY GLORIOUS. Convinced the weather would hold, we packed another load of food for Advance Camp and prepared for a long stay. The rest of the afternoon was spent lazing in the sunshine as the shadows of the peaks lengthened, creeping down the screes and into the valley.

Margaret cooked another of her marvellous three-course meals and in the cool of the evening the six of us set off once more for Advance. Rob and Jeff, who knew that they were not to be on the final ascent, were doing a really terrific job and offered to return to Base the same night. This meant we would be free to go back onto the wall the next day whilst they and Mag made another gruelling trip up to Advance with the third tent and the last of the supplies we would need.

On arrival at our tents, a brief inspection proved them none the worse for wear and we tried to convince ourselves that they were, after all, pitched in a safe position. Rob and Jeff departed down the screes into the long twilight of the Norwegian night and we settled down to sleep. Nick, as usual, went out like a light but with the previous hurtling boulder episode nagging at the back of my mind it was some time before I fell into a restless sleep.

Avalanches were still falling, though much less frequently, from the gullies of Store Trolltind directly behind us. We had learned to accept them like the passage of traffic outside a city house, but it was the boulders that came crashing and ricocheting down the nearby screes at less frequent intervals that really disturbed me. I found it hard to lie there calmly and accept Bill's fatalistic philosophy that 'if they were going to land on the tent, then they would do and there was no point in lying awake listening for them.' As one particularly large boulder rumbled past, obviously only a few yards away, I wondered how it was that Nick too could lie there undisturbed and impervious to the noise. A stoic lot, I thought.

When morning eventually came, the clouds had once more blown up the valley and descended onto the summit of the wall, clutching at the trolls with grey, greedy fingers. I looked out feeling disappointed and saw John likewise peering up from his tent at the dismal skies. Like me, he had again spent most of the night wondering which boulder was going to demolish his tent. We decided that Advance Camp was most definitely not a healthy place to sleep and agreed we should spend as few nights there as possible.

Hoping the weather wouldn't turn to rain we breakfasted and equipped ourselves with a few more fixed ropes. Setting off up the snow we could see the Norwegians too were coming up to renew the attack on their route, but our hopes about the weather were unfortunately short-lived. By the time we reached the foot of the Introductory Wall it had already started to drizzle and the cloud was dropping.

The fixed rope section proved delightfully easy and the ascent of the tape ladder, as expected, posed no particular problem. Beyond this, I led out across another ramp of slabs much more difficult than the first and zigzagged back to a stance above the last belay. We were now on the upper edge of the Introductory Wall and directly below the first of the three sections we had seen from Advance.

Nick came up with the next fixed ropes and I moved off again over easy-angled rock with the bottom edge of the upper snowfield hanging ominously above. It was with some relief that I reached the doubtful protection of a small vertical wall, which would take a couple of good pegs. Nick joined me, and as John and Bill followed, I traversed onto the detached snow slopes on the left, horribly aware that I was now moving out of the frying pan into the fire. Or, should I say, into the firing line.

Feeling like a sitting target for any stones falling from the wall, I moved with what seemed desperate slowness up the snow slope to a small refuge behind a tottering serac. The lower edge of the hanging snowfield from which it had split now leant alarmingly and water gushed out from beneath it down the steep slabs. Thinking it was about time I had some sort of protection, I hammered a blade into a pathetically thin crack. It bent after an inch but with no other choice I clipped the ropes in and set out across the watery holds of the slab.

The rope-drag over the snow slopes below was shocking and with only twenty feet to go to reach the obvious security of the slit below the vertical wall I struggled desperately over the slab. Any moment I expected to hear the unearthly whine of a stone screaming down the wall, but it never happened. I tugged at the ropes, slithering over the slab inches at a time, searching with cold, wet fingers for holds that seemed non-existent. Suddenly the ropes freed themselves and, momentarily out of balance, I slid down the slab only to land improbably on two small footholds, my heart in my mouth. Another move and I was under the overhang. No amount of water dripping from the roof could counteract the longed-for safety it offered. I put three pegs in to make extra sure the fixed ropes were secure and shouted down to Nick, by now invisible in the mist below, that I was across.

As I began to take in the climbing ropes, I knew he was on his way, climbing rapidly up the fixed rope I had left. Across the slab, I could see the end of the blade peg bending as the strain came on it. Once there, with a wary glance upwards into the mist and a tug at the peg to test its security, he took hold of the fixed ropes again and tensioned over the slab to join me below the dripping roof.

John and Bill were hard on our heels and as they had the other fixed ropes in their sacks we set off again to find the route. I was anxious to locate the point where we would have to move onto the vertical wall. It was located below ledges on the wall we had seen on the reconnaissance, where we thought there might be a good bivouac cave. So once again I took the lead.

The line of ascent was obvious. We were now in the slit at the base of the wall and hoped to follow it as far as we were able. Unfortunately it was too narrow for us to squirm up inside it so the climbing was mainly in the bergschrund between the wall and the snowfield, bridging precariously between rock and snow over the dark depths of the crevasse. This continued for two long pitches and only on the latter did the bergschrund become too wide. We were then forced out again onto the open expanse of the snowfield, which was surprisingly steep, almost vertical in places. Reaching its upper edge I was able to move back to a belay point in the slit and Nick soon followed.

Bill and John followed on behind, fixing the ropes up the bergschrund and snowfield before we gathered in the slit to decide our next move. Due to the thick mist it was impossible to see more than twenty feet up the wall but I was sure we should have started up it some distance back down the snow. Cold and wet, we were on the verge of returning when suddenly and obligingly the clouds parted for a brief moment, long enough to see that the bivouac site, if it were such a thing, was only a hundred feet above us, and the way to it was only a few feet back down the slit.

Surprised that it was only one rope-length above our present position we cheered up considerably and took a closer look at the part of the wall that led to our objective. A vertical groove plunged down out of the mists that had once more closed above us, ending in a series of overhangs, which disappeared into the gloomy caverns of the bergschrund. Water, falling in a continual stream from the groove, had bored a huge cylindrical hole into the snow beneath. Its mouth, which was five feet wide, narrowed into dark-green depths. Its sides were fluted with columns of ice, plunging down into a gloomy ice dungeon. To cross this and make any attempt at climbing the overhanging groove would require artificial aid, which takes time, and in cold wet clothes and drizzling rain this wasn't a tempting prospect. Our momentary elation at having seen the bivouac had been well and truly dampened. We wondered who would be bold enough to attempt it.

Nick, in his usual laconic manner, offered to 'have a look'. Belayed on a couple of axes and the pegs in the slit, I let the ropes out as he moved down into the bergschrund. The overhanging base of the groove was just out of reach. Cutting steps up the vertical snow wall of the crevasse, he tried again higher, and then, balancing out from his axe he was just able to touch the rock on the opposite side. Propping himself in this position, bridged over the black, hungry mouth of the hole, he let go of the axe and sorted through the pegs at his waist. The grey mist swirled round us and icy water ran down the groove over his hand and into his sleeve.

Having chosen a peg, he inserted it carefully in a crack in the overhang where the point just gripped. Carefully, he let it go, to reach for the hammer swinging by his side but at the first knock it loosened and fell, dropping down the snow hole. Again he took a peg from his waist and forced it into the crack. Quickly and cautiously he gave it the first gentle tap. It held, the rock biting into the soft metal edges of the channel. Now, tiring with the awkwardness of his position, Nick hammered the peg home and hurriedly snapped in a carabiner and the rope. At last I could help by easing the strain as he clipped in his etriers and swung across over the gap. We were finally on the wall.

Undeterred by the water running down the groove, Nick moved into a standing position. Another two pegs and he was moving over the bulge and onto vertical rock, climbing free and vanishing from time to time in the drifting mist. The ropes moved out smoothly, only stopping when we could hear the noise of a peg being placed, then moving on again. Suddenly he shouted down: 'I'm here! There's a fantastic bivvy – a perfect ledge as dry as a bone with a big roof above.'

This was great news. It must have been the only place on this part of the wall completely sheltered from rain and possible stonefall. At last, our luck was in. All we had to do now was make this section of the route convenient for future ascents. So before leaving to climb up to Nick, I tied on the fixed ropes and some tape etriers. Once over the first tricky move, I was able to thread the tapes into the pegs as I went, leaving a ladder of etriers up the overhanging start.

Up at the belay, we fastened the fixed ropes then, with a grin, Nick escorted me along an easy ledge to the bivouac. It was a terrific place, a flat ledge almost eight feet long by three feet wide, completely protected by a huge roof. Before descending, we pulled all the spare equipment up to the bivouac ledge then fixed the ropes for an abseil. We went down, teetering doubtfully on the lip of the overhang above the black hole before pushing out backwards and dropping to land in a flurry of wet snow on the steep slopes beyond.

Cheered by our find and the fact that we had successfully negotiated the approach route and made our first breach in the wall we set off down the fixed ropes. There was now about one thousand feet in place. Soaked by the rain, we almost ran down it, eager to get back to Advance and some dry clothes. But when we reached the upper edge of the Introductory Wall it had been transformed into a waterfall, which was splashing down in torrents over the ropes.

If any part of us had been dry when we started the descent, it didn't survive the drenching of those last few hundred feet.

When we arrived back on the screes, the Norwegians were just coming down from their route so we wandered across, curious to see how they were managing in the perpetual rain. Leif said: 'We didn't have any diving suits. We've only managed to climb another five feet above our highest point.'

It was obvious what he meant. The whole of their route was streaming with water and if conditions didn't improve they had decided to abandon the climb and start elsewhere. We shared their disappointment as the line they had chosen was superb. Wishing them luck, we departed for our tents, arriving just in time to meet Mag, Rob and Jeff with the extra food and tent. Nick and I claimed the chief cook for our tent and having changed into dry clothes, Mag made the best meal we ever had at Advance.

The first stage, fixing the ropes up the Introductory Wall and onto the wall itself, was complete. We could now start to carry equipment up in preparation for the ascent.

NINE

Equipping the Bivouac

Precipice Team Ready to Start

'Intrepid members of a British expedition expect to start their climb today up the almost vertical face of the 3,300ft Trollveggen – the Troll Wall... they have been held up by poor weather for almost a week. About 200 yards away a Norwegian expedition also last night completed their preparations for their assault on Europe's last unconquered precipice. Earlier it had been believed that the two teams could not make simultaneous starts for fear of accidentally dislodging rocks on the other. But Norwegian sources said last night that the expeditions would start their climbs as far apart as possible. The most critical time would come when the two parties were converging higher up the mountain.'

Daily Express

After another night of hair-raising bombardment that left Mag vowing she would never sleep at Advance again, we started to sort out the equipment for the ascent. We had decided to allow enough food for ten days on the wall for a party of four. The majority of this was dehydrated and concentrated foods and sweets. There were also a few tinned luxury items, most of which would be used at the First Bivouac and some of which would be left there along with other food and dry clothing for use in emergency in case of retreat.

We decided to reduce the number of pegs we would take. During one of the brief glimpses we had of the route from our fixed ropes, we had seen the actual features of the climb. The Great Slab and the Narrow Slab seemed to be the key to the ascent and we felt sure they could be overcome without the use of too much aid. Their angle seemed reasonable and on the Great Slab at least there were definitely good cracklines. Eventually we decided to take an assortment of about two hundred and fifty pegs and thirty wedges, about a quarter of which would probably be needed for belays. We added fifteen bolts for emergencies. These were packed along with seventy alloy carabiners, the hammers, our personal etriers, ten tape etriers, a selection of nuts on cord, two 300-foot climbing ropes and a sack-hauling rope. On top of this was heaped all the essential food, clothing and bivouac gear.

Working on the steep and unstable screes of Advance Camp it was 3 p.m before the six rucksacks were finally ready, each weighing about fifty pounds. By this time, the Norwegians had arrived. Viewing the still dismal weather, they had decided to remove the fixed ropes from their route. We asked where they intended to make their next attempt and they pointed across to the huge dièdres almost opposite our tents.

They had decided on the line we had picked during our winter reconnaissance as an alternative choice. It was a terrific mountaineering route and a great line well worth doing for its own merits. But we still felt that in its upper part it avoided what was, for us, the main challenge – the ascent of the Troll Wall.

Wishing us continued success with our route, they set off across the screes to reclaim their equipment and we decided that, despite the lateness of the day, we might as well carry our gear up to the First Bivouac whilst the weather was fine. The danger of being benighted is non-existent in the Norwegian summer. There is always sufficient light to climb by, whenever you start.

Mag started down the screes for the homely security of Base Camp whilst we shouldered our heavy packs, heading off up the snow slopes to the fixed ropes. Once again, we had hardly reached the bottom of the route when the inevitable drizzle began to fall. We began to wonder if, in fact, the legendary trolls did exist and had some magical control over the weather. By the time we had reached the tapes in the middle of the Introductory Wall, our old friends the waterfalls were back in fine form.

Drenched by the pouring water, we found it impossible to climb the tape etriers with the sacks on, so Nick and I went up with a sack-hauling rope and traversed across to the next belay. Normally this was sheltered, but the platform was now being showered with icy spray from the waterfalls. Since it was also the only place where we could stand to haul the sacks up, we were soon saturated.

Unfortunately, because of our position above an overhang some distance to the right of the previous belay, we found it impossible to pull the sacks directly up to our ledge. The only way to get them to our eyrie was hauling them up the first half of the pitch to the start of the traverse, and then sliding them along the fixed rope. This required someone to belay at a peg in the very middle of one of the streams of water to deal with the changeover. Rob offered to do the job and no one argued.

After what seemed an eternity of pulling and manoeuvring, the six large and heavy sacks were finally heaped on the platform. We stood over them, wet and shivering and wondering what to do next. There was only one sensible decision: cover the sacks with a bivvy sheet and get back down to Base for some dry clothes, a good hot meal and a decent night's sleep. All of us had suffered just about enough wet weather.

Unloaded, we were soon racing back down the snow slopes. With the sleeping bags from Advance stuffed in a spare sack, we rushed on through the endless rain down the screes to Base. The Norwegians were likewise descending after fixing about three hundred feet of rope up the preliminary stages of their new route. Until the weather cleared there was nothing much that any of us could do. Margaret, of course, was glad to see us all back and as it was our first night at Base for three days, she made a special meal for the occasion. Then we turned in for a good night's sleep free from nightmares about falling boulders.

Next morning, the weather seemed to be improving a little, though the clouds were still clinging to the peaks and there were occasional brief showers of rain. Between these, we did our best to dry our clothes by the campfire as Mag set to work cooking another 'Rimmon Special'. By the end of the day, the clouds were definitely breaking. The wind, which had been carrying the unreliable weather in from the sea for the last ten days, was beginning to change direction. By evening, the sky was almost clear. Knowing the wind from the mainland to the southeast often brought good weather we had an early night.

When we woke at eight, it was indeed fine. A small puff of cloud was hanging above the screes, trapped by the cold air in the encircling walls. More were streaming from the summits of nearby peaks but elsewhere the skies were blue. Feeling sure the long-awaited good weather was on the way, we left Mag at Base and set off once more for Advance, almost enjoying the long walk up the screes.

Without packs we reached the tents in just over an hour and set off again up the snow slopes and fixed ropes, relieved to find the sacks were still dry. The waterfalls had lost much of their ferocity and only a small shower was splashing over the slabs beyond. Even with the sacks on, we managed to cross them without getting too wet and then, climbing slowly, we moved up the easy-angled rock above. There was still no sign of recent stonefall from the wall and we were beginning to doubt if our fears had been justified.

The crossing of the slab between the seracs that had given me so much trouble on first acquaintance proved delightfully easy now a rope was in place. The passage up the bergschrund and snowfield was also much simpler and we made good progress to the bottom of the wall below the bivouac.

We had noticed lower down that much of the snow had melted since our last visit three days ago, but we were surprised to find that so much had gone that the lowest tape hanging on the overhanging wall was now almost out of reach. Nick finally managed to grab the lowest loop and swing up gymnastically for the next and before long he was up at the belay near the bivouac.

John and I followed, to help with hauling the sacks up, while Bill, Rob and Jeff sorted the equipment out below, filling all the water bottles and clipping the ropes to the sacks. The first three came up without too much difficulty, though the weight was tremendous. We shuddered to think we would be carrying almost as much for most of the way up the wall. When the fourth sack was halfway up, its carabiner snagged on a projecting piece of rock. It was a costly mistake. The carabiner should have had a screw-gate or been doubled up with another snaplink. As it was, the gate opened and the sack slid off, falling down the wall and straight into the cylindrical hole in the snow at the bottom – a perfect shot.

Bill peered over the edge and said he could just see it jammed in the bottom of the ice-tube, some thirty feet down. He volunteered to be lowered in. Once there, he clipped the sack back onto the hauling rope, this time with two carabiners, their gates on opposite sides, and we eventually pulled it back up to our ledge. We would have to be careful it didn't happen again higher up the wall. A similar mistake would be disastrous.

Removing Bill from the hole proved more difficult. To prusik up was awkward in its lower, narrow confines. Terrible noises issued from its gaping entrance, so we assumed that bridging up the ice-covered walls wasn't much easier. Eventually, with much tugging from above, Bill emerged slipping and cursing from the top gasping for breath, much to everyone's amusement.

The last two sacks and the water bottles were then pulled up to our belay, and Bill followed. Down below, Jeff and Rob, who must have been feeling very envious of us, wished us the best of luck and started the descent of the fixed ropes. As the weather was still good and looked like remaining so, the four of us were now ready to make our attempt at the wall.

We carried the sacks over to the bivouac and began to prepare for our first night. Tomorrow, if the weather held, we would start the climb. If not, well, we would wait here and sit it out for a while. Thanks to the selfless work of Rob and Jeff, we had enough food and equipment with us for ten days of climbing, as well as emergency supplies at this First Bivouac. Relaxed and happy, we tidied the ledge, making it as comfortable as possible, put a few pegs in to belay ourselves for the night and cooked up a large meal on the gas stoves. Then, pulling the bivouac sacks up round our waists, we settled down for a pleasant evening.

Far below, Rob and Jeff were just disappearing down the screes and moving onto the lower snow slopes for a glissade, when high above them there was a deep rumble as one of the still frequent avalanches erupted from the gullies of Store Trolltind. It provided us with the best laugh of the evening, as the two ant-like figures scurried back onto the screes and out of its path. It was only when they finally vanished from view and we had finished our meal and had time to think, that we began to feel the solitude of our position. Already, one thousand feet of climbing was below us. Above, towering into the skyline of large frowning overhangs, was another three thousand feet of unknown rock whose difficulties we could only guess at. The route we would have to take was obvious and frighteningly inescapable, the only real weakness in a sunless world of vertical rock.

Most immediately, the Great Slab stared down at our ledge, ominously large and very wet. A gigantic prow of overhanging rock completely roofed its upper edge and we wondered how we would escape. The only solution seemed by the cracks, which cut their way almost horizontally across the upper edge of the Great Slab and out onto its skyline. Beyond that, we could see little of our proposed route until the sweeping lines of the Narrow Slab curved out to meet the final overhangs. We wondered if it really did lead to the Summit Gully as we had originally thought.

From here it seemed to end in impossible overhangs, the only possible exit seeming to be up an overhanging cleft, which looked extremely difficult and very wet. Not for the first time we wondered how we would get down if it proved impossible, or if one of us were to have an accident, or if the weather were to break – a lot of 'ifs'. Huddled together in the bivouac we felt small and lonely and very apprehensive. Perhaps our critics had been right and we had indeed 'bitten off more than we could chew'.

As the evening drew on, we dozed a little, unable to sleep despite the comfort of the ledge and nagged by worries. We had got a bad dose of the jitters. Meanwhile, the rays of the setting sun glowed red on the peaks across the valley as it sank below the clouds, concealed for the next few hours, yet still throwing a golden light into the night sky.

Between restless periods of sleep, we spent the night looking out across the stark vertical horizon of the wall. A creamy wisp of cloud streamed from the elegant summit of Vengetind to the east, contrasting with the blunt, black, almost ugly monolith of the Romsdalshorn in the foreground. Always our gaze returned apprehensively to the wall. Tomorrow we would be climbing into the unknown.

Part Four

The First
Attempt

TEN

The Nick

Britons' bid to conquer climb

' "The Nick", a 150-foot rock groove named after Tony "Nick" Nicholls was so difficult to climb that 35 steel pegs had to be hammered in to provide holds – and it took Nick a whole hour to fix one of them.'

Peggie Robinson, Daily Express

As the sun broke the horizon to the northeast, the pale glow of the northern night was replaced by dazzling brightness, which penetrated the bivouac sacks with almost instant warmth. It was good to think we might catch a few rays of nourishing, life-giving sun every morning before it slipped behind the wall. Glad to have an excuse to start we cooked a last luxurious breakfast of tinned food and a large sweet brew of tea before repacking the essential equipment into four climbing sacks. Nick and I were to take the lead over this first section, so we roped up, happy to be active and eager to move off.

'This is it lads,' I said as I stepped off the bivouac and onto the wall. The weather was good and we were on our way. After eleven days of frustrating climbing over cold, wet rock and bad snow, in mist and rain, it was a real pleasure to be moving out onto dry clean-cut holds. This was really climbing. The sun had still not disappeared behind the edge of the wall and I was able to appreciate to the full the joys of route finding over steep but not too difficult rock where the body can move in a continuous flow of movement. The ropes behind me curved gracefully across the line of the traverse and I soon reached the base of a groove and belayed.

From the bivouac we had thought this groove might be the easiest method of approach to the Great Slab. Now below it, I wasn't so sure. Where there should have been a crack in the back, there was nothing. It was blind. I called to Nick to come across and on arrival he agreed; it looked hard. Anxious to find the answer to this first section, I decided to lead off again and continue the traverse to the foot of the next dièdre and as I reached its base and gazed upwards it was obvious this was the way.

Although the corner in the back overhung considerably, the whole of the vertical hundred and fifty-foot high left wall was split by a thin wavering crack that had previously been hidden from view. I shouted the good news over to Nick and began to put a few belay pegs in. The ascent of the crack would obviously be time-consuming artificial work and whoever was at the bottom would want a good belay to rest and rely on.

Meanwhile John moved up to Nick and between them they hauled the sacks up to their small stance below the first groove. It was obvious from the language that erupted almost immediately that this aspect of the climb was not going to be fun. By the time Nick and John had joined me and the sacks had been manhandled across the last section of the traverse, it was also obvious that sack-hauling was going to take up almost as much time as the climbing. Nor was the polypropylene rope comfortable on the hands, despite wearing gloves.

It was already midday when we started the dièdre. I led off up the steep cracks, placing pegs with difficulty and balancing up precariously into the top rung of my etriers, each time feeling the peg was about to drop out at any moment. The occasional good placement boosted my confidence and I worked slowly up the crack until, at fifty feet, a small but very inviting foot-ledge appeared to my left. Succumbing to the temptation I strode across and hammered three satisfying belay pegs in up to their hilts. The next hundred feet – obviously difficult – was Nick's problem. He accepted the proposition with a grin and clipped an assortment of hardware onto his belt with obvious relish. Nick was out for the kill.

He came up the pegs with the unhurried speed of experience, climbing past me with nonchalance and the unspoken confidence that exists between two climbers who have done many routes together. Almost immediately the difficulties increased as he moved out over a small overlap. Above, he was silhouetted against the sky and below, the ropes hanging from my belay disappeared from sight past the foot of the groove, leading the eye down over the overhangs to snowfields vertically beneath.

Nick was climbing well and it was strange to think he had never before been on a crag higher than a few hundred feet. He was moving slowly and carefully up the wall, his rate of progress an

Nick, high on his eponymous 'Nick'. *Photo: John Amatt*

indication of the difficulty of the pitch. The only noises were the tapping of his hammer and oaths muttered as the peg placements worsened. Occasionally he would call out brief instructions: 'Watch it now. Another bad peg. It's only in about an inch.' Then he would balance upwards, a silhouette attached to the lifeline of the ropes but otherwise in a world of his own, conscious only of the few feet of rock immediately around him. Instructions floated down again: 'Hold it! The peg's moving.' Then a moment's silence. 'No, it's stopped. I think I can see a good crack higher up. I'll have to stand on the peg.'

And so it went on as Nick led out higher and higher up the dièdre. Belayed, hung from pegs, and half expecting him to become detached from the rock at any moment if one of his pegs came out, I prepared myself for the upward pull of the ropes caused by his downward plunge. Miraculously the pegs stayed in and Nick's spider-like movement continued steadily and with painstaking care until, only twenty feet from the top of the dièdre, he reached an impasse.

The crack, which had been fading all the way up the wall, had finally disappeared. The last few pegs had been so poor that Nick had only been able to use them as handholds to aid his progress, unwilling to trust his weight to them. Now, balanced in a precarious and tiring position over a hundred feet above me, it took him an hour of patient searching, trying peg after peg in every possible niche before he finally inserted his last insecure point of protection. With the peg in, he thought he could see a way off round the left arête and, using the ropes for tension, he traversed delicately out in a superb position, a small figure on the skyline.

Down below me, John and Bill, tied securely to their belay pegs, had been passing the time by reading but now, sensing the silent tension in the atmosphere, they craned their heads up to watch Nick tip-toeing out onto the lip of the comer. He moved round out of sight and the hammering resumed. Then, looking back over the top, he said, 'Cracked it! There's a good ledge about thirty feet away.'

The ropes began to move out smoothly and with more certainty, and then going up in quick jerks. Nick had clearly reached the ledge and was taking the rope in. I prepared to move off, nervous about leaving the security of my belay for the loose pegs above and waiting for the ropes to tighten before starting.

Above me, the pegs hung from the crack, more out than in, and the higher I climbed the worse they became. Each peg had to be tested cautiously, but despite this, one suddenly came out on me just below the traverse-line. Not surprised, I grasped the comforting ropes above, firmly held by Nick, and regained balance almost at once. I wondered how Nick, who must have been even more aware of their looseness than I was, had managed to continue his calm progress, whilst expecting to part company with the rock at any moment. Reassured by the ropes, I moved onto the small holds of the traverse, then balanced out across the wall to a tiny stance on the arête. Not far away, on a large ledge, I could see Nick grinning fiendishly. I said, 'That's a terrific lead, mate. You must be bloody barmy.'

His grin widened. Eager to reach the obvious comfort of the ledge after half a day spent on vertical rock, I traversed across the final section to Nick. Above, an easy wall led to another ledge on the very top of the dièdre. Since it offered a better position to haul the sacks, I continued up to this next stance before belaying. Nick came up to me, and once again we experienced the arm-straining torture of sack-hauling. The four sacks, each of which weighed around fifty pounds, were dragged slowly but surely up the hundred and fifty feet of vertical rock, each inch being a victory for tired and aching muscles. At long last we grasped the final sack and clipped it to the belay, only then realising that the shadows of the mountaintops were lengthening as the sun sank towards the horizon, bringing cool air across the wall. I looked at my watch. It was past nine o'clock. We had been climbing for sixteen hours.

Bill came up next. At halfway, there was a tug on the rope; another of Nick's pegs had come out. He finally arrived bursting with congratulations about Nick's lead. Without further ado we decided that this first very impressive obstacle should be called The Nick. Then it was John's turn, and as he started, Nick began the ascent of the wall above our belay, which we knew would bring us to a snow ledge at the foot of the Great Slab. He led it with ease and I followed up onto a patch of sloping snow.

Ahead there seemed to be a better platform, but dominating everything, and appalling in its sudden close proximity was the Great Slab. Only this slab was not a slab. Looking at a slab face on always makes the angle seem steeper. But even allowing for that, the slab was in reality a wall, a massive wall soaring up in one tremendous sweep to the great overhanging prow above. Its outer edge leant inwards, creating the illusion of an easy angle, whereas in truth its verticality hardly relented over the whole of its awe-inspiring three hundred feet. Below it a deeply etched groove plunged down, ending in space high above the darkly shadowed screes. Confronted with this gigantic sweep of rock I felt pathetically small and inadequate. Even Nick, who was never intimidated, seemed visibly impressed.

Still, to continue boggling at the thing wasn't finding us a place to sleep, so I traversed the snow slope to the platform at its end. It was small, but once the snow was levelled it would be adequate for the night. I called across to Nick, and he brought John up. Between them, they hauled the sacks up to their belay whilst I stamped and scraped the snow into position for our second bivouac. By the time we were all on the ledge and in the bivouac sacks it was after midnight and we were more than ready for the long-awaited brew made from melted snow, and the meal that followed.

Tired though we were, we felt elated at the thought of the difficulties we had just overcome, thanks to Nick's tremendous lead, but the thought of the sack-hauling yet to come depressed us. We had already suffered enough of that punishment. We wondered why it had never occurred to us to bring a pulley. After all, we knew they were used regularly on the big vertical and overhanging walls of the Dolomites and Yosemite. Not to bring one when we knew we would have so much equipment to haul was obviously a big mistake but there was nothing we could do about it.

Resigned to the situation, we huddled together in the sacks. It was nearly two o'clock, the coldest part of the night. The Great Wall, as we had now started to call it, Great Slab being a definite misnomer, loomed ominously above us. Faced with this vast, oppressive wall of rock I once again felt puny and insignificant. Even its inanimate indifference to our presence seemed somehow to emanate a distinctly hostile challenge. This was a psychological pressure I think we all felt and which none of us had experienced before to such an overwhelming extent. The Great Wall was an enemy.

We tried to keep it from our minds and, tiredness triumphing over fear of the unknown, slowly fell into a deep, undisturbed sleep.

Eleven

The Great Wall

Climbers in ropes

'Two British mountain climbers went to bed tonight on the side of a vertical 3,300-foot wall suspended by ropes in specially made rucksacks... trying to scale Europe's most inhospitable mountain face...'

Yorkshire Post, with no suggestion of why there were only two climbers.

IT WAS NINE O'CLOCK BEFORE WE AWOKE on the third day, suddenly aware that we had overslept and that the Great Wall was still leering down at us in what was, to my mind, sadistic anticipation. We stretched cramped muscles, cold from the bivouac on damp snow, and began to cook breakfast.

Down below in the valley, we saw with some apprehension that the wind had changed. A heavy mass of cloud was rolling up the fjord from the sea, blanketing the valleys from view and surging over each freshly gained ridge like steam brimming over a witch's cauldron. The amusing thought that perhaps it was the trolls brewing up some bad weather gave us little satisfaction. As we sorted out the equipment to resume the ascent, we could only hope the clouds would disperse in the heat of the day and were not a prelude to a break in the weather.

I started across a delightfully fingery traverse, which brought me to a stance near the inner edge of the Great Wall and at the upper end of the huge groove that plunged down into the now appreciable depths. Nick and John followed, leaving Bill to finish packing the equipment at the bivouac. With no option but to get the ball rolling I started on the next pitch, where I would clearly get to grips with our oppressive adversary.

An obvious crack rising from the groove some twenty feet below us split the whole of its length and once gained would give the only feasible route. I climbed down, facing outwards in the groove using tension from the rope, and managed to place the first peg, hammering it as hard as I could into the heart of the crack. The attack had begun.

I clipped my etriers in and swung onto the wall, then once more started the relentless process of artificial climbing, a kind of warfare to which almost everything must yield. The crack was steep and its centre portion was both loose and overhanging. We began to realise just how wrong we had been when we had called this a slab. Above, the angle relented slightly but even then it was only just on the right side of vertical. It was, however, sufficient to allow me to place pegs more widely apart before laybacking up to a conveniently situated belay ledge. It was small but enough for two to stand in comfort.

After hauling the sacks across to their belay, John came up to me, one of the pegs in the loose section coming out in the process, and then led off up the next section of the crack. Now steep and solid, it gashed the wall for almost two hundred feet. Dwarfed by the awesome savageness of overhanging rock that hemmed us in, he led up using hardly any aid. His progress was made all the more difficult by the impressive assortment of hardware it was essential to carry on these long pitches where no belay ledges were visible and any amount of aid might be required. Only the belts specially designed for the purpose made it possible to carry a good assortment of equipment and helped to make the weight bearable.

Placing wedges and pegs as sparsely as possible, John continued up the crack, which widened, cutting its way through an overlap in the wall. The ropes moved out smoothly and evenly and as he became silhouetted high above and apparently near the top of this section, I began to hope another pitch might see us off the Great Wall. Then a shout came down. He could see a small ledge. Everything seemed to be going fine. We weren't climbing fast, but at least we were making steady progress.

Using a few more pegs he eventually reached the ledge and belayed. I could still see almost the whole of the soles of his boots, and realised just how small the ledge must be. Leaving him to arrange himself in comfort, I brought Nick up to my stance and between us we once more began the agonising task of sack-hauling. As each numbing weight arrived, the amount of space available for us on the ledge shrank, making it yet more difficult to pull the next one up.

I was so exhausted with the effort that when we finally had all four sacks on the ledge I decided to attempt to climb up to John carrying mine with me. Foolishly, I thought this would be easier than hauling it whereas in practice it proved even more futile and tiring. It took all my strength and much pulling from John to heave both myself and the sack up the pitch. When at last I tottered up the final few pegs and saw the belay ledge, I knew I hadn't underestimated its size. The whole of this part of the wall was vertical and the stance was merely a sloping scoop in the rock a few inches wide. To make matters worse, our belay consisted of a wooden wedge in a crack that was too awkward a shape to fit anything else, and a large nut. Neither looked very secure.

Nevertheless, John, who had put them in, seemed to think they were perfectly sound. Preferring to believe him rather than think about the possible consequences if he was wrong, I clipped in alongside him and took my sack off, hanging it from the wedge. Gasping up the last pitch with the weight of the sack tugging downwards at my shoulders as I fought up every move had been,

Left NW Face of Reka. Photo taken after overnight ascent of groove-line right of summit in snowstorm in 1962. *Photo: Tony Howard Top right* The peaks of Raudtind on the island of Hinnøy, Vesteralen. The 'Red Blade' follows the ridge-line leading to the second summit from left. *Photo: Sigurd Skjegstad Middle right* View past the Hurtigruten coastal ferry to the Lofoten island of Austvagøy, with the 'Alpine' peaks of Trakta and Store Trolltind, left of centre, traversed in 1962. *Photo: Snorre E. Aske Bottom* SE Face of Reka on the island of Langøy, Vesteralen, first climbed in 1965 by left-hand groove-line after the ascent of the Troll Wall. *Photo: Reidar Larssen Overleaf* Left to right: The Three Pillars of Breitind, Semletind and Trollryggen with the Troll Wall in shadow below the latter, and the highest peak, Store Trolltind, on the far right. *Photo: Tony Howard*

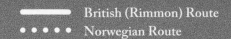

British (Rimmon) Route
Norwegian Route

Summit Gully

Exit Chimney

Narrow Slab

Central Basin
Flake Crack
Black Cleft

The Canyon

The Great Wall

The Nick

Eagle's Nest

First Bivouac

Intro
Wall

Opposite The Troll Wall showing the lines of the Norwegian Route (dotted) and Rimmon Route. *Photo: John Amatt Top left* Tony Howard enjoying the sun at the top of the Troll Wall (original Troll leather waistbelt behind). *Photo John Amatt Top right* Bill Tweedale, immediately after being knocked unconscious by falling rocks in a thunderstorm on Semletind East Pillar. His helmet was split open and is now on backwards over a bandage. *Photo: Tony Howard Bottom left* Tony 'Nick' Nicholls. *Photo: Amatt/Howard Bottom right* John Amatt, gazing pensively up at the Narrow Slab. *Photo: Tony Howard*

Top Another rainy day at Base Camp, only good for humping gear to Advance, or washing hair! Bill, John, Nick, Rob, Jeff, Maggie and Tony doing exactly that. *Photo: Amatt/Howard Bottom* Preparing at Advance Camp. *Photo: John Amatt Opposite* Bill avoiding suffocation in the bivvy tent. *Photo: Tony Howard*

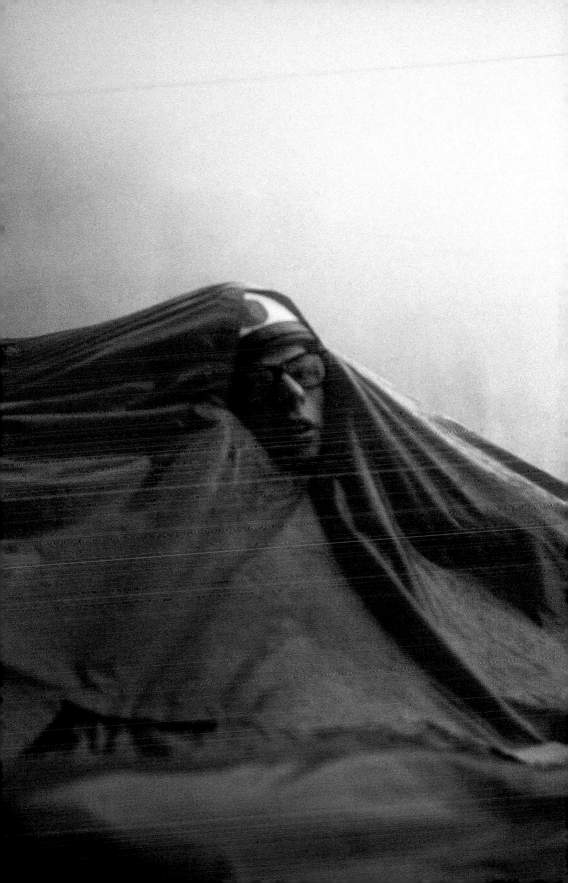

Opposite Preparing to retreat after the first attempt. *Photo: John Amatt Top left* The misery of the retreat. *Photo: John Amatt Right* Tony on the first pitch of The Nick. *Photo: John Amatt Bottom left* John at the bivouac below the Narrow Slab. *Photo: Tony Howard*

Top left Tony on the Flake Crack at dawn. *Photo: John Amatt Top right* Looking down the Narrow Slab. *Photo: John Amatt Bottom* Bill, John and Tony on the summit of the Troll Wall. *Photo: Amatt/Howard Opposite* Tony embarking on the wet and overhanging Exit Chimney. *Photo: John Amatt*

Top left The Norwegian Team: Jon Teigland, Odd Eliassen, Ole Daniel Enersen and Leif Norman Patterson. *Photo: Leif Norman Patterson Top right* Ole. *Photo: Leif Norman Patterson Middle left* Old timers: forty years on, Jon, Odd and Ole below the Troll Wall in 2005. *Photo: Iver Gjelstenli Bottom* Odd jumaring high on the Norwegian Route. *Photo: Leif Norman Patterson Opposite* Going, going, gone – the Rimmon Route bites the dust in the big rockfall of 1998. *Photo: Harald Sæterøy*

Top left Tony on the first ascent of the SE Spur of Norafjell, 1967. *Photo: Rob Holt* *Top right* The North Face of Semletind, first ascent by John Amatt and Rusty Baillie in 1967. *Photo: Tony Howard* *Bottom left* On the approach to Ingolffjeld's South Face, Greenland. *Photo: Tony Howard* *Bottom right* Ingolffjeld's 2,000m South Face during heavy snowfall – Bill and Tony were up there. *Photo: Tony Howard*

Top left Exploring the Hidan Canyon. One of many superb canyon trips in Jordan. *Photo: Di Taylor*
Top right The South Face of Iharen in the Hoggar Mountains of Saharan Algeria, where Tony and Mick Shaw climbed the Kohlmann-Dufourmantelle route, directly up basalt columns to the summit. *Photo: Tony Howard Bottom* The superb Rock Bridge in the forbidden Farayid Mountains on Egypt's Red Sea coast. *Photo: Di Taylor*

Top The magnificent walls of Tsaranoro, Andringitra National Park, Madagascar. *Photo: Tony Howard*
Bottom left Ethiopian shepherd boy, Simien Mountains. His only possessions a few rags and some smouldering charcoal wrapped in cow dung. *Photo: Di Taylor Bottom right* One of many first ascents in Wadi Rum, southern Jordan, an area discovered by Tony and friends in 1984. *Photo: Tony Howard*

John Amatt on the Great Wall with a large rack of wedges. *Photo: Tony Howard*

for me, just about the limit. I gratefully accepted John's offer to continue in the lead.

He moved back onto the last pegs and regained the crack, once more climbing free in a superb position. Below, the clouds from the valley, which was now hidden from view by the angle of the wall, were creeping into sight. The weather was obviously worsening. Grey fingers of mist were groping towards us and overhead the sky was almost overcast. In the shadow of the wall it was becoming cold and damp. Almost a hundred feet below, I could see that Bill had joined Nick and the two figures were curled together in their duvets between the jumble of sacks.

Above me, John was still climbing steadily, pausing occasionally to place a peg or dislodge loose stones jammed in the crack, which were barring his progress. He threw them off into space and they went spinning dizzily past, crashing only once in the giant chute formed by the huge groove below the Great Wall, before howling off into space to be swallowed up by the mist below. It was horribly unnerving to watch and I cast an uncertain eye at the belay, whose security I still half-doubted.

Time was passing, mostly absorbed by the laborious process of sack-hauling. If we didn't escape from the Great Wall soon, we would be trapped on the open face without any protection from the weather or anywhere to sleep. Furthermore, knowing there were snow ledges above, we had very little water with us and my thirst was growing powerfully.

Still John moved up, and eventually he reached a small black depression large enough to belay in, once more almost a hundred feet above me. 'How far to the top of the Great Wall now?' I asked. Surely it couldn't be far, as he was at the start of the diagonal cracks that led out below the prow to its left edge. I saw him lean out, gazing upwards, then the answer came down: 'It might be another hundred feet yet. I can't say how hard it'll be, but it doesn't look too bad.'

The mist was still hanging furtively round the bottom edge of the Great Wall as if undecided about its next move. There was still a chance we could get to a ledge before the bad weather set in. If only we didn't have those blasted sacks. Hoping for the best, I took in the ropes that hung down to Nick. Below, the two white-helmeted figures bobbed into activity as they re-arranged themselves and then Nick moved up into the crack.

He was just reappearing through the gash in the small overhang when one of the threaded chockstones pulled out. Suddenly off-balance, he went swinging backwards, out over a thousand feet of space. For one brief moment he was silhouetted against the grey swirling mist before swinging back onto the rock on the end of my rope. 'Thanks, mate,' he said, and the event was over. Had this happened to the leader it might have proved disastrous; now it was nothing more than a passing incident. Unperturbed by his brief flight in space, Nick continued upwards and was soon beside me, looking with equal distaste at the belay. 'Is it okay?' he asked, warily. 'It is so far,' I replied with a grin, and once more we began hauling the sacks up from Bill, struggling as they jammed and snagged on every projection.

Stood with only the toes of our boots on the minute ledge and now completely dependent on the security of the belay, we were from the start hampered by my sack hanging beside us. When the next sack and then the third came up, it was almost impossible to move. Each bag was hung onto the dubious wedge. Even wearing gloves, the ropes cut painfully into our hands and lifting the fourth sack up those hundred feet of rock seemed to take an eternity. At last, with our hands sore and cramped into a clenched position we clipped it in alongside us. Time had flown. We had been on the Great Wall almost fourteen hours and it was after midnight.

As I started up the next pitch to John, the mist was now beginning to rise up stealthily. Below me, Bill was already hidden from view. The ropes hanging down from Nick simply vanished into the mist. This had swallowed Bill whole and seemed to be closing malevolently around us. The pitch was hard, and when I arrived at John's small stance I was greeted by water dripping remorselessly down from the huge prow, now also hidden in the mist above. John was huddled dismally in his anorak, which was thoroughly soaked, and I tried to shelter unsuccessfully beneath a small overhang beside him. The mist was everywhere and we were completely shut off in our own small world, only able to see a few feet on either side. It was almost two in the morning. Bill, who had been on his small ledge for half the day, was now invisible almost two hundred feet below and must have been feeling very lonely. Nick too was now isolated and out of sight, hanging with the sacks from the wedge, whilst above our heads, the crack still continued, slanting out left, black and wet into the mist.

Its difficulties were unknown, and to start it now, tired as we were and not knowing the outcome, would be futile. As if to emphasise the impossibility of our situation, it was starting to rain, a cold saturating drizzle. We began to shiver. A decision had to be made. We would have to go down, there was no other choice. After all the toil, after all the graft, after almost reaching the top of this most coveted section of the route, which we felt sure was the key to the lower half of the climb, we had to go down. The decision was obvious but the words were hard to say.

We stood for a while in the rain wondering if, after all, there was another way out. But the decision had to be made, abseil pegs had to be placed and we had to start on the descent. The Great Wall, which had impressed us so much, had won. Having made the decision, I doubted very much if I would ever return.

TWELVE

Retreat and Despair

Blizzard beats Britons' bid to conquer climb

'Four Lancashire lads walked wearily down a mountainside here today, soaked to the skin and very tired. They had left the unconquered wall to the Norwegian party that has been trying to race them to the top. But the young men promised they would be back. For four days and nights they had fought their way up the 3,000ft precipice that is the last big unclimbed north wall in Europe... a blinding blizzard turned ledges into snowfields and rock faces into waterfalls. For 36 hours the battering went on [and they] decided they must retreat.'

Peggie Robinson, Daily Express

UTTERLY DEPRESSED BY OUR DEFEAT AND THE DRIZZLING RAIN, we began to prepare for the descent. I shouted down to Nick, 'It's no good. We'll have to go down.'

His silence was sufficient answer. We hung the abseil ropes down into mist, their ends hanging over the grey void. In the misery of our failure I looked regretfully at the untouched crack above; it would retain its secrets. The wall beyond would remain a mystery. I gave it one last glance, thinking I should never again be at such close quarters, and then, as I was still roped to Nick, I started the descent, cautiously moving down into the mist.

95

Down into the drizzle, alone in a grey claustrophobic world of half-light, my only contact with the others being the ropes that disappeared above to John anxiously watching the abseil pegs, and below to Nick carefully taking in my climbing rope.

He loomed up out of the mist some distance to my right and I pendulumed across, helped by a firm pull. With resignation, I tied back into the belay. Now we had to start lowering the sacks back down. What a waste of effort it had all been. Words were superfluous.

Lowering them to Bill should have been comparatively simple, but tired both physically and mentally, the task proved almost impossible. The ropes tangled maddeningly or hooked themselves round the descending sacks when they were only a few feet from Bill. Every sack had to be hauled back up to our tiny stance two or three times before we finally succeeded in lowering it to Bill, with hands raw and weary from constant effort.

I shudder to think how long it took us to lower those four sacks. We had been active for twenty hours and I had ceased to worry about the safety of the wedge or about the vile drizzling weather and our cold, wet clothes. When the sacks jammed and we had to lift them agonisingly back, my forearms seemed to be bursting with pain. We would close our eyes and pull, and pull, and pull until the strain of the sacks became too great, a strain from which there was no release, as the weight of the sacks was too great to hold for more than a few moments in our exhausted state. Slowly, our shoulders would sag and our backs begin to buckle; the ropes would begin to slide out through our hands and once more we would start to pull, pull, pull. Then the sack would be free of the infuriating tangle of ropes and we could let it slide, the rope, with its course prickly fibres, running through burning fingers, down to Bill.

At last – at long last – the rucksacks were down and I followed them, abseiling off from the one wooden wedge, leaving Nick belayed on the nut. John followed, appearing out of the mist and drizzle and, finally, Nick abseiled off again, down to the bottom

John Amatt descending the Great Wall, engulfed by the storm during the retreat. *Photo: Tony Howard*

of the Great Wall, eager now that our old bivouac site on the snow platform was so near. The routine of sack lowering began again, and then back we went along the traverse. At eight in the morning, after twenty-three hours on the go, we were once more at the bivouac. It had been, as The Beatles said, a hard day's night.

Inside the bivvy sacks we lay together in our damp clothes for warmth. Remembering the old adage, 'when in doubt, brew up,' we lit the stoves and scraped some snow up from outside to make a drink, almost falling asleep in the hot stuffiness of the sacks as the snow melted and finally came to the boil. Unable to touch the hot metal of the pans with our tender fingers we had to keep our wet gloves on whilst we lay back, sipping slowly at the hot sweet tea and feeling its warmth move down into our stomachs.

In the gloomy world of mist and dripping rock, barely lit by the greyness outside, the drizzle was turning to sleet. Large drops of wet snow were falling onto the bivvy sacks and drifting past into the void below. We closed the flaps and listened to the snow splashing over our heads. Inside, it soon became cold and wet with condensation. Moisture trickled down onto our duvets and trousers, and our damp clothes stuck clammily to our skin. The cold wetness of the snow platform penetrated the sacks and before long, puddles began to form in the bottom.

We lay there, dozing, finding it difficult to breath in the small, enclosed confines of the sacks, and becoming colder each moment. In our sack, Nick and I lit the stove, almost choking in the instantaneous dry heat but then, after a few minutes, the flames began to burn low and flicker. They finally went out and we woke up stupidly from our half-doze, realising that we no longer had any oxygen.

We opened the flaps again and stuck our heads out, sucking in a lungful of cold, damp air. The sleet was still drifting down, forming in wet heaps on the ledges and in the hollows of the bivvy sack. We reached out, scraping some up to make some soup. In the other sack, Bill and John were trying to light their stove, but with the flaps shut they couldn't even strike a match, so little fresh air was present. We couldn't help but laugh as they suddenly stuck their heads out, just as we had done, gasping for oxygen.

All that day, the weather remained the same and we lay dozing in the sacks, only the smallest of gaps kept open for fresh air. The condensation was becoming worse and all our clothing was thoroughly soaked. Nevertheless, having rested and eaten, we were once again feeling a return of the confidence that we had lost with our defeat and the nightmare of descent. Now, staring up at the black, oppressive, mist-shrouded mass of the Great Wall we knew we could climb it; we knew we had been within a hair's breadth of success. We also knew we would have to try again for our peace of mind. We had been too close to let it go without another try.

Even in our present isolated position a thousand feet up the wall, cold, wet and wrapped in mist and falling snow, we were beginning to think of our next attempt. I wondered what was driving our minds to go back up into the unknown again, when barely twelve hours ago we had been overwhelmed by the misery of failure. Then, we had wanted nothing but to go down, to get off the wall. We still had to go down anyway, as we no longer had any dry clothing in which to face up to what could be another week of climbing but now our minds were beginning to scheme and plan again. The grim struggles of the night were being pushed into the background as returning hope that we may yet succeed began to fill us with the enthusiasm we had lost.

The attempt had not been wasted. A third of the route had been climbed and the pegs were in place. Furthermore, we could leave the equipment up here at the bivouac and the sack-hauling rope could be left in place down The Nick as a fixed rope. Though that had its problems. The great advantage of our fixed ropes was that, being polypropylene, they were incredibly light. In fact they were so light they could float, but they weren't designed for shock loading, so were far from suitable for holding a fall, something that was definitely possible on Nick's pegs. More cheering than anything else was the thought that for the next effort we could bring a pulley. Despite our present position and the terrible weather, we were beginning to feel better as the bitterness of our defeat was replaced by the pleasure of anticipation. Now we had something positive to think about rather than failure.

Yet the day still passed slowly and dragged on into the long cold night. The puddle in the bottom of the sacks grew deeper; the material was glistening wet with water, which trickled in everywhere. We began to shiver relentlessly in our wet clothes and lighting the stove for brief intervals only served to emphasise the damp chill that returned immediately. We slept rarely, unable to rest because of our discomfort, whilst outside in the cloud-wrapped night the sleet was turning into snow, falling thickly everywhere. Streams of water were running from the rock, dripping from the overhangs and splashing noisily onto the sacks. It continued throughout the night and it was obvious if we were going to get down alive we would have to start the next day, whatever the weather.

The morning light hardly penetrated the thick gloom of mist and we lay in the bivouac lethargic, suffering from hypothermia and unable to rouse ourselves to make the effort of descent. We cooked a breakfast of porridge followed by the inevitable brew, eagerly clutching the cans of tea in our wet, gloved hands. Even so, the bouts of shivering which shook our bodies continued. We knew that we had to start down immediately whilst we were still able. Moving sluggishly, uncomfortable in our soaked clothes, we crawled out of the sacks into the sleet that was still falling. With frozen fingers we sorted the equipment out, leaving almost all of it on the ledge under the sodden bivouac sacks before starting on the descent. This was our commitment to return.

Concentrating carefully on each problem to avoid a potentially disastrous mistake, we traversed back to the top of The Nick, every move hampered by the clinging wetness of our clothes. Our hands gripped numbly onto holds deep in wet, slushy snow. It was a slow and painful process and when we arrived above the dièdre we spent ages stood in the sleet trying to place suitable pegs for the abseil. None of the cracks were good. Finally, we had to manage with three loose pegs tied together in opposition.

Someone had to go first, so I slung the ropes round me and stepped over the edge gingerly, the grit-clogged rope cutting painfully through my gloves and rasping like an endless file across my wet fingers. The pegs held. Feeling that my cold, numbed hands were going to lose their grip on the rope, I had to stop repeatedly before plucking up sufficient courage to start once more on the painful descent. The others, now lost above me in the mist, followed likewise with agonising slowness until we were all four together again and ready to begin the traverse back to the First Bivouac.

The snow was piling deeper on the ledges and a waterfall dropping vertically from the summit was crashing down the groove that separated us from the shelter of the ledge. I moved across towards it, now completely unable to feel my fingers, worn almost to the flesh. Placing them on the snow-covered rock, I hoped that they would hold, but could feel nothing. Traversing through the waterfall seemed impossible. Three times I moved into its icy torrent, each time forced back almost unable to breathe as the force of the ice and grit-filled deluge battered down on me from 3,000 feet above.

Within fifty feet of the fixed ropes and bivouac where we had food and dry clothes, I had to give up. I moved slowly back across the ledges and Nick offered to have a try. Aware of the pain he must be feeling I watched him move out and disappear under the bitter onslaught of the waterfall. He clung there grimly for ages, defying the drenching assault of the freezing water and then suddenly the ropes started to move again. He was through.

He fastened the rope across as a fixed line and we followed as quickly as possible, hand over hand through the waterfall and along to the First Bivouac. We rubbed ourselves down briskly, changing into dry clothes and eating some of the food we had left there for just such an emergency. What did it matter that we would get wet again going down the fixed ropes? At least now we were warm and dry and could feel life returning. Our hands and feet, which had been wet and numb for over twenty four hours, were tingling with fire.

The whole of the wall was still swathed in mist as we abseiled off down to the snowfield. The victorious trolls standing aloof on the summit were hidden from view. Below us, the fixed ropes were likewise concealed by the swirling clouds. But now we had reached them, the descent was swift and simple. We hurried down almost without noticing our torn fingers, but leaving trails of blood on the ropes. All of us had only one thought: we were down and tonight we would be in warm, dry sleeping-bags with one of Mag's large hot meals inside us. The wall would have to wait till the weather improved before we returned. The trolls had won round one, but next time we wouldn't fail.

Part Five

The Final
Ascent

THIRTEEN

Good Weather and High Hopes

Rimmon six return for a rest

'A British expedition returned to base today after climbing nearly halfway up the 3,300 foot "unclimbable Troll Wall"... Norwegian experts said the British team are in high spirits... In seven days they reached a point 1,350 feet up the wall. They have had to drill holes to fasten their bolts because there are almost no fissures in the mountainside for footholds or bolts...'

Bolting confusion in the **Oldham Evening Chronicle**. In fact, none were used.

WHEN WE WOKE AT NOON THE NEXT DAY, the weather had started to improve again and the wind was no longer blowing from the sea. The clouds had also lifted from the wall and even we were amazed to see the amount of snow that had fallen in the last two days. Once again, the summit trolls were glistening virgin white in the sunshine. In the dark shadow of the wall every ledge had a thick covering of snow.

Almost a thousand feet up the route the Norwegians had finally chosen, a small red tent was just visible through the binoculars. It was pitched on a large ledge – almost a meadow. According to Mag, Bill and Jeff, Leif and Jon had put it up just before the bad weather started. It was on the lip of one of the steepest sections of their route. They must have done some excellent climbing.

The Norwegians had fixed ropes up to the tent and Odd and Ole were intending to set off with the last of the provisions. Leif and Jon had stayed up there during the storm, managing to sit it out. Unlike us, they were reasonably protected by their bivouac tent and location. It probably helped having a walkie-talkie radio to keep in contact with their Base. It must have given them a psychological advantage; it can be very reassuring to speak with friends on the ground, not just for the human contact, but to keep up to date with weather forecasts and what's happening. On the other hand, it seems to me this contact with the outside world changes the whole spirit of a climb, robbing the climbers of the essence of being there, alone and committed on the wall, making them less self-reliant. Perhaps I'm too much of a purist, or technophobe.

Despite all my reservations, the two Norwegian girls, Helene Olsen and Rotraut Hofmann, who were staying with the climbers visited our camp in the afternoon and we had the pleasure of talking to Leif and Jon on the wall.

'Hello Trollveggen. Hello Trollveggen. This is the English Base Camp. Are you receiving me? Over.'

Leif's voice came back in reply, crackling loudly through the speaker. He was full of questions about our route and why we had come down. They had apparently managed to weather the storm very well and if good conditions continued in the morning they hoped to make a start on the next stage of their route up to the snow ledge on the East Pillar. We told him of our complete wash-out at our bivouac and said we planned to resume our ascent as soon as the weather permitted. We wished each other luck, before the sets were turned off, returning Leif and Jon to the isolation of their bivouac into which we had intruded for a few brief minutes. Once again, they would be alone in a world of vertical rock, our tents merely two white specks in the valley below.

Meanwhile, Odd and Ole would be well on their way up their

fixed ropes and the weather was still improving. Already the snow on the summit was starting to melt and hardly a cloud was visible in the sky. We pulled our sleeping bags and airbeds outside into the sun and rested aching muscles and sore hands. Our wet clothing, draped over the branches of the trees and across the tents, was steaming and drying quickly in the heat. High above, the black wetness of the wall was becoming striped with patches of dry, grey rock as the streams of melting snow began to disappear. If only the weather would hold, the wall would soon be in perfect condition again. Rested and rejuvenated, we were more eager than ever to get back on the climb after our failed first attempt.

We had learned a lesson and now had an opportunity to remedy the mistake, a mistake that should never have happened. In the morning we would go to Åndalsnes and buy a pulley. Our hands were still very sore, especially Nick's, as he had done a superhuman job, not only sack-hauling and lowering on the Great Wall, but also on descent through the waterfalls. With another day of rest we hoped all four of us would be fit again, so with nothing better to do, we turned in early, after a perfect day of idleness.

Next day dawned without a cloud in the sky and the screes shimmered in the early morning heat. The towering ramparts of the wall blazed in the few hours of light granted to its northern aspect and up there, in the small red tent, the Norwegians were preparing to climb, taking advantage of the sun's friendly life-giving warmth.

They made progress throughout the day, heading for the huge, darkly shadowed dièdre that would bring them out into sunshine again on the East Pillar. There they would have plenty of snow for their bivouac and, should it prove necessary, a line of escape up the East Pillar climb. Such is the size of the wall, however, that looking up from our camp through binoculars we found it almost impossible to spot them. We could only envy them their situation, high up and alone, masters of their environment, looking down on the world below.

At noon we left for Åndalsnes to get the pulley. Armed with this new weapon we could begin to think of sack-hauling without so much apprehension. The town was filled with tourists, eagerly purchasing binoculars and travelling up Romsdal on coaches specially organised by the hotels, to watch 'the climbers'. The newspapers were all full of the story of the 'Race on Trollveggen', and the local photographer's shop window displayed a huge picture of the wall. On it were marked the respective routes and the points reached by both parties, and everyone was speculating who would 'win'. Even our obviously unhurried wanderings round town in the sunshine couldn't convince them we were not intent on 'racing to the summit'.

We returned to camp in the evening, the proud new owners of a two-inch single-wheel ship's pulley and repacked what little equipment we had brought down from the climb. Tomorrow, if the weather was still fine, we would have to start again. More than a few days of good weather was too much to expect and we had to make the best of any opportunity. With this in mind, we did justice to another of Mag's wonderful meals and once again had an early night.

The skies stayed clear, and a few stars shone to the south, just visible on the darker horizon. To the north and overhead, the pale blue vault was still lit faintly by the rays of the sun that rose with dazzling brightness in the morning, tempting us up out of our sleeping bags. Hardly a streak of wetness could be seen on the wall and the screes, surrounded by towering peaks, would soon be a furnace. We ate a breakfast of fresh fruit and decided to wait until the heat of the day had passed before starting on our second attempt.

Nick's hands were still extremely sore, and much as he must have wanted to go with us he decided against it, feeling he would be unable to climb safely or help with the sack-hauling. We assured him that the three of us would be able to manage the sacks now we had the pulley, and that he should definitely come. He was, however, adamant and insisted he wasn't going to be a liability to us on the ascent. That was typical of Nick.

We would have liked to have waited until his hands improved, as he had done so much of the hard leading on the first attempt as well as getting us down through the waterfalls, but the weather was far too unreliable to delay. We had wasted two days of the best weather already and another could be vital. As the sun disappeared behind the peaks in the late afternoon, John, Bill and I left reluctantly without him. Considering the fact that the weather broke into a thunderstorm only hours after we completed the climb five and a half days later, it is possible we would never have reached the summit or got down safely had we delayed another day.

It felt for us, as it must have for Nick, a sad departure as we set off through the woods. I felt badly at having to make the decision to leave without him. Those staying at Base Camp all wished us luck and we finally turned our backs on the tents and set off again for the wall, already feeling the apprehension of the unknown. We knew if we failed this time we would probably never return. This was it.

Carrying only a little equipment, we scrambled easily up the screes, once again below the dominating shadow of the wall, reaching Advance Camp as evening approached. Pleased to see it still undamaged, we stopped for a rest and to make some soup, finally deciding not to continue up to the First Bivouac that night but to snatch a few hours sleep where we were and start early in the morning.

Maybe our decision was really prompted by an unspoken desire to stay on terra firma as long as possible. Whatever the reason, we cooked a good meal and after talking for a while, lay down, each of us determined to get what sleep we could before once more moving onto the wall. Each of us lay silently, assuming the others were asleep, whilst in reality we were all thinking about the all too recent nightmare of our retreat. Nagging little thoughts were continually running through my mind: 'I wonder what that crack's like at the top of the Great Wall? Have we allowed enough food for emergencies? I wonder if there'll be enough water higher up?

Should we take a few more bolts? Suppose the weather breaks when we're high on the wall? Suppose one of us has a serious accident? What if we can't get down?' I wished I was back at Base with Nick.

Tormented by fears of all that might happen, I wondered how John and Bill could sleep so peacefully. Neither of them had moved for ages. Then, suddenly, my train of thought came to an abrupt halt as a huge boulder came crashing wildly down the screes, hurtling straight for us. I was startled into frenzied activity, leaping instantly for the tent door. John and Bill, it turned out, were no less alert. Our three horrified faces peered out into the night just as the enormous rock bounced past. Spinning crazily as it flew through the air, it bounced on the screes lower down in a cloud of dust and smoke before ricocheting off once more in its mad plunge down the mountainside.

We looked at each other with nervous grins and crawled back into the tent. Bill said, 'I don't know about you two, but I haven't slept a wink.'

'Me neither,' I replied. 'In fact, I've just about scared myself to death with thinking about the climb.' It felt like an admission.

'Me too,' said John. 'I thought you were both sound asleep. Neither of you has moved all night.'

The ice was broken, and we were happy to be talking instead of secretly worrying about the problems that lay in wait for us. Bill said, 'I'll be glad when we get started. I've spent half the night trying to work out an excuse to go back down.'

John and I laughed, knowing we both felt the same and glad that Bill had the courage to say it. Now we knew none of us would go down. We were committed. The wall was a challenge, a personal challenge, we had been dreaming of climbing it for six months. The rest of the team had done everything possible to get us this far. Turning our backs on it wasn't an option.

Happy to be discussing our hopes and fears, we talked for quite a while and made ourselves some soup to pass the time on. It was just past midnight when, finally, feeling more at ease, we dropped off into a brief sleep, only to be woken again by another boulder crashing past. I asked Bill the time. It was 2.30 a.m. 'How about getting started?' I said. Despite our poor night's rest none of us felt tired and we were eager to be off. Too much adrenalin, or perhaps the two days of rest and rich living at Base had done us good.

'Suits me,' said John. Bill was obviously as keen. We cooked some beans and had a large brew can of tea each, remembering the long thirsty day on the Great Wall on our last attempt. A little after three we were ready to start. The night was crisp and clear and the snow slopes below the Introductory Wall glowed palely in the faint light. We stamped some life into our chilled feet and set off once more for the wall. The nervous apprehensions of the night had gone and we kicked our way up the snow slopes with eager anticipation. The time for worrying was over. We were on our way.

FOURTEEN

The First Day

Sleeping out on the 6,000 foot wall.

'Six lads and a lassie from Lancashire are becoming the big attraction for tourists here. Hotels are running trips for Americans to peer through binoculars from the valley to pick out the tiny dots that are the boys tackling the Trolltind Wall, the last unconquered north wall in Europe.'
Peggie Robinson, Daily Express

As we were carrying hardly any equipment we soon reached the fixed ropes, already having taken off our duvets despite an almost frosty chill in the pre-dawn air. We moved out onto the Introductory Wall, and roped up where it steepened, past the tapes and up the pitch above, both now almost completely dry. Moving together we continued up the easy pitch onto the snow slopes which had caused so many anxious moments when we were fixing the ropes almost two weeks ago. Now, with the ease of familiarity, we were able to cross over to the slit at the foot of the wall and almost run up the fixed ropes above, arriving at the pitch below the First Bivouac.

Already, the sun had burst over the horizon bringing instant heat, quickly dispelling the haze that lay over the distant peaks and throwing the ribs and grooves of the wall into bold relief. For the next two or three hours we would be able to appreciate its warmth until it vanished behind the silhouette of the wall, plunging us once more into the shadow of north-face isolation.

Above us, the tapes that had been so heroically fixed in place by Nick during the bad weather were now far out of reach; the snow, from which he had climbed across so precariously, had now melted away. Even the bottom loop of the tape was far beyond my grasp. Fortunately, we had also left a fixed rope hanging down the pitch so I was able to knot some loops into the bottom of this. Using these it was just possible to swing up across the bergschrund and grab the bottom loop of the tape etriers. I pulled up fiercely, my feet flailing in space, and managed to reach the next loop. Holding this I could then bring my feet up into the bottom loop and rest, after which the remainder of the pitch was straightforward. Before long we were all up at the First Bivouac.

Taking the opportunity to enjoy what was left of our day's quota of sunshine, we sat down and helped ourselves to a large tin of

John, Bill and Tony back at the first bivouac on the second attempt. *Photo: John Amatt*

beans out of the stockpile at the bivouac. We ate them cold and found them deliciously refreshing after the sweaty struggle up the overhangs in the morning sunshine. Bill lay back relaxed, smoking a cigarette as if he had no cares in the world, whilst above us the Great Wall frowned down, once again massive and dominating.

I wondered what lay in store for us this time but also looked forward to the Narrow Slab high above, scything its way so cleanly through the overhangs. Right now, only the Great Wall worried me, and I for one would be relieved when we overcame this particular obstacle. John and Bill, however, seemed content to be lying in the sun, so I savoured the brief respite for a while longer until, after packing a few extra provisions from the bivouac, I set off again along the traverse.

Just as I was leaving, we heard a yodel echoing across the wall shattering the silence. We all looked up, startled. Just visible on the very edge of the wall, silhouetted against the sunlit background of the Romsdalshorn, were the four tiny figures of the Norwegians. They were at the top of the huge dièdre above their old bivouac site and had presumably spent the previous night on the large snow platform on the East Pillar. We could see them waving and waved back. Somehow it was good to know there were other people on the wall. We envied them climbing the rest of their route in sunshine for most of the day, because they were no longer on the north face. We could already see the shadows creeping towards us.

Giving them another wave, I resumed the traverse towards The Nick. The waterfalls that had forced me back on our descent only four days ago had disappeared and the climbing was so pleasant that the fixed rope placed by Nick and now hanging pitifully across the rough, dry rock was almost a mockery. It was amazing to think that such an enjoyable and comparatively easy traverse had almost been a death trap when we last had to cross it. What a pity Nick couldn't be with us now, as he deserved to be.

As I was first on the rope, it would be my task to lead The Nick, a thought which I found a little frightening; I had been gripped enough just going up it as the second man. I set off feeling doubtful about the outcome, but gaining psychological reassurance from the fact our sack-hauling rope was hanging down the vertical wall and might come in useful. I needn't have worried. Once underway on the pegs I had placed on the first pitch, I felt my confidence returning. My etriers jangled in their familiar way and the walls of the dièdre led my eye up to the sweeping overhangs on the still sunlit upper wall. Memories flooded back of glorious climbs on the sun-drenched cliffs of the Dolomites, subduing my fears as I climbed from peg to peg, no longer concerned by the increasing exposure.

Running the pitches together, I reached the worsening pegs placed so carefully by Nick and judiciously knotted a loop into the sack-hauling rope, which was hanging nearby, clipping my rope into it to act as a running belay. Although I still had little faith that the polypropylene line would hold a fall, it had to be better protection than Nick had on his ascent, or so I convinced myself as I climbed on, up and out across the exposed traverse to the edge of the dièdre, marvelling again at Nick's superb lead.

Once above The Nick, I fixed the pulley to the belay and shouted down that I was ready to haul the sacks up. This was the moment we had been waiting for. If the pulley worked, we could forget completely the grim struggles that had ensued after each pitch on our first attempt. I clipped the continuous three hundred foot loop of line through the device while below me, John and Bill attached the first sack. Positioning myself to feed the rope round the pulley, I called down to them to start pulling. The sack fairly flew up the wall; it worked better than we had ever hoped. If only we had brought it on our first attempt.

The three sacks were at my belay in a matter of moments. All three of us were overjoyed at the simplicity of the method and cursed ourselves for not remembering to bring one before. Bill romped up the pitch, and John followed with equal speed, all amazed by our fast progress. The morning was little more than half gone and already we had covered what had previously been almost a day's climbing. By noon we were at our Second Bivouac below the Great Wall. At the back of the ledge was the bivouac sack we had left, covering the food and equipment, and on the ledge itself a little snow remained.

We now had a problem. Our intention had been to bivouac here tonight and make an early start on the Great Wall, but as it was only midday and we had only been climbing for eight hours we were tempted to continue. I, for one, had spent enough time sat on this ledge, staring up at the Great Wall. It had impressed itself upon me so much that it had, for me, become the psychological key to the whole route. As long as I was beneath it, it worried me, and until I had climbed it I would be unable to rest. I felt sure that once we had overcome this section, we would be able to tackle anything else with complete confidence. I suggested continuing to Bill and John, doubtful about their reaction, thinking they might still prefer to bivouac here and start early the next day. But to my surprise they agreed wholeheartedly. It turned out they felt exactly the same way about the psychological barrier of the Great Wall.

Not knowing when we would next have a plentiful supply of water for a drink or a good ledge to bivvy on, we decided to stop for a while and make some soup. The sky was an unbroken dome of blue and the scree and snow slopes visible far below shimmered in the midday heat. Even in the shadow of the wall it was warm and we were able to leave our duvets packed in our sacks. I even began to sense a feeling of anticipation for the battle we were about to rejoin with our old opponent. The Great Wall still threw down its blatant challenge, but this time we were prepared for it. This time we wouldn't turn back.

Once the soup was finished, our excuse for inactivity was gone. We shared the equipment out evenly amongst the four sacks, clipping much of the pegging gear to our harnesses, partly to lessen the weight of the packs, but mainly so we would be prepared for any eventuality. If it was to be war, at least we would be well-armed.

John led off across the traverse to the groove at the foot of the wall and then, when the sacks were across, Bill and I followed. Once again I moved down into the huge groove and out onto the pegs. I had led this pitch before, and knowing its problems was able to climb quickly. The almost pleasant routine of sack-hauling followed, then John came up, ready to get to grips with the two pitches he had led previously, which would bring us to our previous high point.

Like me, he knew the difficulties he would be encountering, and with all the pegs in place he was soon high above at the small stance with its wedge belay. Things were going well, and with growing confidence I brought Bill up to my stance, the same one he had spent almost a day on during our earlier abortive attempt. Between us we pulled on the rope and sent the sacks flying up to John. It was almost inconceivable how the pulley had transformed the nightmare of sack-hauling and lowering that Nick and I had experienced on this pitch.

At each pull, the sacks spun upwards and as they reached John, hanging from his small belay, we held the rope, keeping the sacks in position until he had clipped them to the wedge. It was then only a matter of fastening another sack onto the loop of rope and resuming the operation. Once all the sacks had been pulled up I set off up the tremendous crackline that splits the Great Wall and which John had led so well. Last time, hampered by a heavy sack, I had found it a desperate struggle and had been pulled up every inch of it. Now, I was able to enjoy to the full the niceties of climbing this superb wall of rock surrounded so dramatically by impossible overhangs which dropped away so impressively to the screes below. It was a fabulous pitch, with excellent hand-jams and protected every now and then by wedges or pegs. Only a few were needed for aid.

The crack continued above for another hundred feet, ending at the black, wet stance below the huge prow, from which we had been forced to abseil in bad weather on our first attempt. I joined John at the wedge belay and he led off up this final pitch to the stance. Above was the unknown. If we could force the escape pitch off the Great Wall, we would be able to bivouac in peace.

Seeing John in position at the belay, Bill came up to me on my minute stance and once more, carefully and systematically, we sorted through the confusion of slings holding the sacks and us in place. Unclipping the sacks one at a time, we hauled them up to John. Despite our good progress the afternoon had passed and by the time I reached John it was, as on the previous occasion, almost midnight. This time, however, we had climbed all the way from Advance Camp in one push, and the weather was superb. There was no cold, grey mist swirling stealthily up towards us, or drizzling rain falling from a cloudy sky that obscured the light. The skies were clear, and to the north, the fiery glow of the midnight sun was blood red beyond the distant peaks. A cool night breeze whispered over the rock and the only wetness was from water still dripping silently from the black profile of the overhanging prow above.

Beneath this prow was the escape pitch, a ragged crack rising gently across the upper rim of the Great Wall to a small ledge visible on its outer edge. This was the crack we had seen from the First Bivouac so many days ago, the crack I had thought I would never see again when we had abseiled off in frustration on our previous attempt. Below it, the wall plunged vertically down into the void, to the snow slopes visible in the half-light over a thousand feet below. This would be my pitch. John had led the last two hundred feet of climbing and there was no room on the small stance for Bill to come up and lead through.

Down below, he must have seen us leaning out, anxiously scanning the crack to judge its difficulties. 'How's it look?' he shouted up. 'Hard to say,' I replied. 'I can't really see it properly but it looks like aid-climbing so it might take some time.'

Like us, Bill was no doubt sick of being stuck on the Great Wall in the middle of the night, but without complaint he made himself as comfortable as possible on the small stance where the ledge, sloping down into space, was hardly large enough for both feet.

John also settled himself in, sheltering as well as he could from the slow relentless drip of water falling from the prow. I prepared to start. It was after midnight and twenty one hours since we had left Advance.

Determined not to be beaten by this last pitch, I moved off the belay and immediately had to start pegging across a tilted slab. Above this was a small overhang and then the final crack. As the dripping water trickled down the rock in the growing chill of night, my fingers began to feel the cold. I reached the edge of the slab and with searching fingers felt anxiously round the overhang. It was loose.

I chose a peg from the belt at my waist and prodded it carefully into a crevice in the crumbling rock. It seemed to hold, but as I tapped it gently with my hammer, the rock on either side fell away. I tried again and again without luck in various cracks and began to lose hope; surely we weren't beaten already. There were cracks so there must be a way. It was after midnight, and here I was pottering about in a half-hearted manner getting nowhere at all. 'Come on, Howard,' I said to myself. Then, aloud, I called back to John. 'I can't get a peg to hold. I'll have to try and tension a bit farther out left.'

'Okay, got you,' he shouted to reassure me. The ropes slid gently out for a foot, allowing me to lean a little further round the bulge. Trusting the ropes, I stretched out and jammed the peg again into the loose cracks of the overhang. This time it seemed to grip better. I gave it a knock with the hammer. It held. I hammered it into the crumbling rock and clipped an etrier in. 'Okay John, I'm moving up.'

The ropes eased out again and I stepped across onto the peg. Another few feet had been gained. Further patient searching with cold wet fingers in the loose, bulging rocks to the left revealed another place for a peg and eventually I was able to move up into the crack. But I was dismayed to find it was choked with moss and quartzite and no matter how much I struggled, I couldn't get another peg to hold. I was tired and rapidly losing patience, frustrated by how close we were to success. On the verge of retreat, I noticed a spidery thin crack above. It would just have to take a peg; it was our only chance.

I sorted through the mass of equipment for the smallest, thinnest blade and inserted it carefully. Its razor-thin tip fitted perfectly and the metal sang as I hammered it in. We weren't beaten yet. And so it went on, each time I felt sure there was no place for a peg, just as I was about to give up, something would hold. Nevertheless, at two o'clock and after making little more than thirty feet of progress, I reached what seemed to be a complete impasse. The crack still continued and the upper edge of the Great Wall was only thirty feet away, but nothing would hold. I tried every trick I knew, but still every peg came out.

Mentally and physically exhausted and thinking I might be able to reason more clearly in the morning, I returned to my last safe peg some fifteen feet from John and settled down in etriers for the night. 'It'll go in morning,' I said with false confidence. 'I might feel a bit better after a rest.'

John pulled the duvets out of the sacks, and Bill and I, almost a hundred and fifty feet apart, pulled them to us on the ropes, before settling down at our uncomfortable belays for the night, me in my etriers, John and Bill on their small foot ledges. Once again we had been on the go for twenty three hours.

FIFTEEN

The Second Day

'A yodel from 18-year-old Bill Tweedale 1,200ft up the Trolltind Wall ended fears that he had fallen. Sightseers with binoculars had reported seeing something fall.'
Unknown newspaper, story entirely false.

THAT NIGHT, CONCEALED AS WE WERE by the profile of the Great Wall, the rest of the team were unable to see us from Base and since Nick knew from experience there was no bivouac site on the Great Wall, they were in some doubt as to our whereabouts.

The Norwegians on the other hand were just visible from Base through binoculars. They were now five hundred feet above the snowfield on the East Pillar and had found a good bivouac site on the edge of the wall for their seventh night. We, on the other hand, partly through trying to climb too far in one day, but mostly because we wouldn't be beaten by the Great Wall, which was both a mental and physical barrier, were in a far less pleasant situation.

Unprotected by bivouac sacks, the cold of the night on the open face was acute. Each of us was shaken frequently by uncontrollable fits of shivering. We nibbled occasionally at the fruit bars, raisins, glucose and chocolate we had in our pockets and dozed at rare intervals only to waken again in a few moments, cramped and shivering. Each one of us was isolated, attached to the others only by the rope and alone with his thoughts. No one spoke, in case by some miracle the others were sleeping. The only sign of life would be the occasional jangle of an etrier or tug of a rope as one of us rubbed cold hands or stretched cramped muscles, desperate to ease the discomfort of their position. All else was silent and still.

I relaxed as best I could hanging in my etriers, resting my head on the rock and trying to bury myself in my duvet. Water dripped regularly onto the hood or trickled down the damp rock and soaked into my trousers. Slowly the cold wetness seeped through and the shivering became worse. Our water bottles were inaccessible in the sacks, but I was so desperate for a drink, I sucked some of the water off the rock with my parched lips, and alternately nibbled a fruit bar, chewing it slowly, trying to relieve the thirst and hunger that was gnawing at my throat and stomach.

Unable to sleep, I looked out at the pale clear skies to the north, and to the distant peaks hiding the sun, which held the promise of so much warmth and life. It was skimming just out of sight behind the black mountains which concealed its longed-for radiance. Above the summits, only the glowing sky revealed its slowly moving arc. Soon it would be dawn. I closed my eyes, weary of watching and waiting and tried again to sleep.

I must have dozed for a while, for I woke to the sun on my face. I opened drowsy eyes to see the splendour of the sunrise. It was five in the morning. I yawned and stretched, rubbing the sleep from my eyes and had another bite of a fruit bar. My thirst was terrible. I looked back down the ropes to John, just below, and to Bill far away down the Great Wall. Both of them seemed to be sleeping. 'Are you awake, John?' I said quietly, not wanting to disturb him, but anxious to be on the move again. A grunt came back in reply.

'I think I'll have another bash,' I said, 'while the sun's still on the wall.'

'Right-oh,' said John, 'I've got you.' And with the sun in my face I moved off onto the shaky pegs to see if I could do any better than the previous night. The pitch had to be overcome if we were to succeed. There was no other way up. At least I was now climbing in the sunshine, and the rock was no longer cold. I reached my previous high point and resumed the patient search of the loose rock filling the crack. There had to be a place for a peg in there somewhere.

Finally, I managed to place a channel peg, battering it in until it had almost disappeared. It still moved when I put my weight on it, but there was nothing else for it. It just had to hold. I stepped across onto it and the peg shifted a little and then stopped. My confidence in it grew as I became occupied with searching for a spot to place the next peg.

Somehow everything stayed where it was, each peg managing to hold my weight as I slowly worked my way towards the wall's upper edge, no longer aware of the sickening drop below or the thirst and hunger that had tormented me during the night. My whole being was concentrated on reaching the small ledge that perched so temptingly on the edge of the Great Wall. Relentlessly I worked at the choked crack, hammering the pegs and clipping the ropes and etriers in and out of carabiners like an automaton. The sun blazed down, warming my hands, and sweat began to trickle from under my helmet, stinging my eyes and filling my mouth with the taste of salt.

As the sun disappeared behind the profile of the Great Wall at eight o'clock, I reached the ledge. I hammered in a belay peg, took off my duvet and equipment, and relaxed. The Great Wall had been beaten. I felt sure now there would be no stopping us.

I rested awhile with closed eyes, almost falling asleep in the pleasant warmth, but then became suddenly aware that drips of water were splashing nearby. My throat was parched, my dry tongue stuck to the roof of my mouth but when I looked up I saw sunlit jewels of water forming slowly, provocatively, on the huge overhanging prow twenty feet above, glittering like diamonds in the early morning sun. Never was a fortune more desired.

The drops swelled larger and larger and then, suddenly released from the trickles from which they were formed, they would plummet into space. I sat on my small ledge, mouth wide open, awaiting these gifts from the gods, moving my head to catch them in flight and each time revelling in the exquisite, heavy, cold splash of moisture as the drops burst in my mouth or on the dry skin of my face.

Down on the Great Wall, Bill was climbing up to John, glad to be off his minute stance and moving again. When he arrived at John's belay, the two of them were able to pull the sacks up to me through the pulley I had fixed at my belay. Then John set off towards me. One of the pegs came out but he reached me without mishap and Bill followed. Before noon we were all together again on the small ledge and ready to move off into the unknown, now aware that an abseil descent would no longer be easy after the long traverse of the last pitch.

John led off, climbing free on more pleasantly angled rock. The time-consuming routine of artificial work was over, at least for a while. He reached a belay out on the main face of the wall itself and we soon joined him again, once more able to see the valley and the two white dots of Base Camp far below. There was no sign of the Norwegian party and we thought they would already be near the top, though in reality they were only a little higher than us, having found some unexpectedly hard climbing barring their way up the edge of the East Pillar, on the exposed lip of the wall.

We packed our duvets back into the sacks and I climbed past John, delighting in the easy natural movement, unhampered by cumbersome clothing or heavy equipment. Above, I could see an obvious groove, but remembered seeing the shadow of a deep chimney cast on the wall when looking up from Advance. This chimney, I knew, led up towards the Central Basin, which was our halfway mark and covered in snow. I had called it The Black Cleft.

Traversing left, I found it less than a hundred feet away, hidden by the bulging wall, and was able to continue up it for the full length of the rope, bridging pleasantly across its walls to a ledge near its top. This was more like it. Now we were really moving, despite our hunger and tiredness. John and Bill pulled the sacks up to me and followed up the chimney before I started again on a short and nasty overhanging crack. My hands were only a few feet from the top but holds for my feet were non-existent and I struggled in vain. I asked John for a shoulder, and he obliged whilst I trampled all over him in a desperate effort to reach some holds. Eventually I stood on his outstretched hand and finally gasped my way over the bulge. Only then did I realise how tired I really was.

They pulled the sacks up again and climbed up the sack-hauling rope to join me. To our left was a small ledge, less than two feet wide, but quite long and the biggest we had seen since leaving the bottom of the Great Wall. Less than two hundred feet above was the bottom of the Central Basin with its permanent little snowfield, below which a superb flake crack cleft the vertical wall.

Its ascent would obviously not be easy in our tired and hungry condition so, after a day and a half of climbing with little sleep and not much to eat, we decided to rest on the ledge and break into the luxury supplies of tinned food. Two tins of steak in mouth-watering gravy and a tin of vegetables in tempting juice were emptied into the pans. We warmed them on the stove, feeling our stomachs churning emptily as the aroma of cooking filled the air. Savouring each mouthful of delicious, refreshing liquid, chewing slowly on the meat and vegetables, we appreciated every tiny morsel and licked every last drop from the pans.

Now, feeling the benefit of our meal, we looked up again at the Flake Crack with similar relish. It looked a superb piece of climbing and one that would be better appreciated after a good night's sleep. Bill spotted a ledge on its right some thirty feet above and we wondered if it would be any better for a bivouac than the rather meagre one we were already on.

I climbed up to have a look, and on reaching it was amazed to see it was a tremendous platform, over five square feet and protected by a small overhang. Then, unbelievably, I heard the unmistakable drip of water and on looking closer saw liquid dripping from emerald green moss in the corner. What more could we want. It was a north wall dream home.

Unable to contain my excitement I shouted down the news to Bill and John. They packed the sacks, sending the pans up in the first, and as soon as it arrived on the ledge I took them out and put them under the drops. As water splashed in, it made music in the tins. No symphony has ever been better appreciated than the happy tinkle of those few drops.

Bill and John came up as quickly as possible, eager to see this palace with running water. By the time they arrived both pans were already half full. Laughing and joking we gulped the cold refreshing liquid into our still-dry throats and put the pans back under the drips to refill whilst we tidied up the ledge for our first decent bivouac on this attempt.

Once in the bivvy sacks, we lit the stove to make a brew and sat back contented and at ease, nibbling at cheese and flatbread and feeling relaxation seep through our bodies. We had been active for forty hours with only three hours' attempted sleep. We knew we had given our best in what had been our greatest, most sustained effort so far. The Great Wall that had preyed on our minds defeating us mentally since we had first seen it at close quarters eight days ago had been climbed. It had been hard and costly, but we had won through.

Now, the climbing was a pleasure and our minds were at rest. We looked forward to tackling the beautiful Flake Crack that soared above us and, whilst we sipped at our tea, we pondered about the Narrow Slab and the problems it might have in store. This time, we felt sure we were right about its angle. Unlike the Great Wall, this slab definitely was a slab.

From the luxurious comfort of our bivouac site we could see it only three hundred feet above us, a long slanting gash surrounded by some of the largest overhangs we had ever seen. Only the exit through these overhangs puzzled us. Did the slab continue the whole way up to the Summit Gully, or would we have to escape by the obvious and very impressive long, overhanging crack that cut through the overhangs? It didn't look easy, but once that problem was solved the route would be ours. No doubt in another three days or so we would find out. For the moment, we were interested only in drinking and sleeping.

We made another brew of tea and then, lying back in absolute contentment, sipped it slowly, savouring the warm, sweet liquid, as the golden rays of the sun lit the northern skies.

Sixteen

The Third Day

Daring 5,300 foot ascent in snowstorm

'Norwegian climbers said the [English] expedition was one of the most daring ever made in the Norwegian mountains. The last 1,500 feet were completed in a raging snowstorm. Norwegians said the final route to the top was extremely difficult.'

A snowstorm fantasy from the **Manchester Evening News**

PERCHED ON OUR THRONE HIGH ABOVE the world we slept like kings, warm and comfortable, our thirst quenched and our stomachs full. A few stars shone feebly overhead, their brightness lost in the glow of the Norwegian night. Somewhere on the East Pillar their flickering light would be falling on Leif, Jon, Odd and Ole, curled up in their bivouac. Or perhaps they had already reached the top?

Down in the gloom of the valley, the distant roar of the river's icy water reverberated against the ramparts of the wall, lulling us as it echoed around the corrie. From between the two white specks that were the tents at Base Camp, a faint blue-grey wisp of wood smoke curled up lazily into the still night air. In the tents the others were sound asleep, their minds at ease. They had spotted the small red dot of our bivouac sack almost 2,000 feet up the face. They knew we had made good progress and that all was well.

Night passed and the few stars faded overhead as the sun began to rise towards the horizon, lighting the elegant snow-capped peak of Vengetind with the first glow of early morning. The luxurious warmth penetrated our bivouac sack and I stretched idly in the sunlight, flexing my muscles to the tips of my outstretched fingers and toes. I rubbed my eyes and looked out at the beautiful world around us. A ring of high peaks glittered in the morning sun while the deep-set valleys far below still slept in the shadow of night. Unwilling to move from the luxury of my bed I reached out an arm for the stove and the pans of water. Having turned on the stove, which roared happily, I took off my duvet to use as a backrest, leaned back and dozed in the sunshine. This was the life – breakfast in bed and not a care in the world.

As the brew boiled, I woke John and Bill and we made two pans full of porridge for breakfast and then followed them with another brew and some marmalade and flatbread. This was really living. Now I felt able to take on the world. Assuming we didn't have to go down, our grim struggles on the Great Wall were now a part of the distant past. And retreat was far from our minds.

Breakfast over, we packed unhurriedly as the sun rose towards the Romsdalshorn. Roping up for the Flake Crack, I had the feeling you sometimes get when setting out for a big climb that today was going to be one of those days when anything is possible. The rock was clean, warm and dry, soaring up towards the overhangs, the upper end of the crack curling over like the crest of a wave. I grasped its edges with confidence, feeling the rough crystals of rock rasping on my fingers, and laybacked and jammed up a pitch more than worthy of any gritstone crag.

Below the upper overhang I knocked in a peg for protection and swung out over the roof to the ledge above. With ease and confidence I began to move left along the ledge, holding a huge block for balance. It moved. It rolled out suddenly towards me, forcing me over the edge. With a feeling of horror I pushed desperately on the block as I tottered on the brim of the wall.

It rocked back, as easily as it had moved forwards. It was larger than a tent, and I regarded it with a shudder before continuing past with infinite care to find an equally comfortable belay without a killer block on it.

The sacks came up next, swinging through space from the bivouac and then John and Bill followed, each of them treating the immense block with care. It looked safe enough, but with the touch of a finger would begin to rock ominously. Still, no harm was done, and a near miss couldn't counteract our light-heartedness as we gathered at the belay now only twenty feet from the bottom edge of our halfway mark – the Central Basin. It was to be twenty feet of hard climbing up a vertical crack either too narrow or too wide to jam and where no other holds existed.

In true 1950s style, I jammed a chockstone in and managed to stand on that, then once more made use of John's shoulders and hands as I struggled up the short, frustrating pitch. Sweating and cursing I swarmed over the top, more through necessity than technique. Still puffing and out of breath, I belayed and brought the sacks up. After that, it was my turn to sit back and laugh as John and Bill grunted and heaved their way towards me.

Above us, the angle of the rock relented and we were able to climb easily up into the hollow in the very centre of the wall where the winter's snow, trapped in almost perpetual shadow, still lay deeply against the rock. We boggled at how many gallons of tea and soup it would make. The memory of our desperate thirst on the Great Wall still lingered.

Crossing the bottom edge of the snow slope, we viewed with respect the awesome, captivating beauty of the Narrow Slab cleaving a slender curving path through otherwise impregnable overhangs. This was, we hoped, our pathway to freedom. The left edge was overhanging, while on its right and above, the wall bulged steeply, ending in huge roofs that hid the upper face from view. If we were right, the Narrow Slab was our way out – the only way out – a slender blade of rock, its outer edge jagged like the teeth of a giant saw and undercut by enormous roofs beneath which the vertical wall plunged down for two thousand feet to the screes. Its superb situation and architecture were breathtaking. We stood there amazed at the audacity of the route that lay before us.

From the top of the snow we climbed up a short crack to a pedestal of rock at the very foot of the slab. Everything was perfect. The sheltering overhangs above, the snow only a few feet away for water, the flat-topped pedestal just large enough for three to sit back in comfort, and a spike nearby to hang the equipment on. The skies were still clear with not a cloud in sight and above all, the magnificent Narrow Slab swept away up into the blue. It seemed that the gods, the trolls and everything else were with us.

It was only three o'clock, but overcome by our good fortune we decided to stop and have a brew. Opposite, the ragged shadows of the trolls that capped the wall, behind which the sun was now passing, spread themselves across the South Face of Store Trolltind, stretching down into the valley, reaching towards the tents of Base Camp. Even here on the wall, in the heart of the almost perpetual shadow, we were warm and could sit back in comfort.

We ate some flatbread and idly considered climbing part way up the Narrow Slab and fixing a rope to give us an early start in the morning. We were still considering it two brews later but no one seemed anxious to start. Our mood was too easy and relaxed to worry about such a minor detail as saving time. Instead, we sorted out some food for a meal and spent a luxurious evening in the bivouac sacks, chatting idly about matters of total irrelevance.

After three days on the wall we were able to treat our phenomenal surroundings with relaxed indifference. Life was becoming a pleasant routine of eating, drinking, sleeping and climbing. It seemed as though we had always lived this way and always would. There was nothing urgent or dramatic about it, no pressing demand to reach the summit, or craving to return to the valley, no worries about what might lie ahead, or if the weather would break. We simply woke in the morning, cooked breakfast and started climbing. That our bed was perched on the lip of an ever-increasing void no longer occurred to us as unusual. When an appropriate ledge was reached, it was merely a matter of stopping climbing, having a meal and going to sleep. Why hurry? We were enjoying ourselves.

From our perch, we watched the shadows of the trolls smother the campsite like tentacles before creeping their way across the valley and crawling up the steep western slopes of the Romsdalshorn. Then we curled up for the night in warm companionship and fell into an untroubled sleep.

Seventeen

The Fourth Day

The hell of the Trolltind Wall

'Overhangs, intense cold, snow, rain, loose rock… and some of the most dangerous and difficult climbing ever done. They had them all… From their bivouacs they watched huge boulders "drift away in the wind"…'

More over-enthusiastic reportage in the **Manchester Evening News**

WE WOKE EARLY AND WATCHED the kaleidoscope of dawn invade the skies before having breakfast in the heat of the morning sun whilst discussing plans for the day. None of us thought it would be possible to reach the Summit Gully at the top of the Narrow Slab before nightfall and unless we did, we could see no possible place for a bivouac. After the lesson of the Great Wall we decided to play it safe and just concentrate on covering the first three hundred feet of the slab. We would then haul the sacks up and return to our present bivouac, leaving the sack-hauling line in place as a fixed rope. This was a pleasant sort of programme since it meant each of us would be able to have a rest at the bivouac while the other two climbed.

Bill led off first, climbing carefully over a precarious 'skin' of blocks poised one above the other and covering the base of the slab. Soon he reached a belay on its outer edge, on the very brink of the huge saw-toothed overhangs with nothing but space below. I climbed up to him and continued over the blocks towards the inner corner where the slab started to sweep out leftwards through the overhangs like a gigantic scimitar. Amidst such inspiring architecture, it seemed desecration to use pegs but the climbing became increasingly difficult. Reluctantly, I hammered in the first and then, with more pegs for aid up the edge, moved delightfully out across the slab, revelling in my position.

Eventually I reached a small stance, large enough for both feet, and hammered in a couple of belay pegs. That was me done for the day. The next pitch would be John's and would likely be as far as we got before evening, although the slab had so far proved much easier than we had expected. I had a last look round before preparing the ropes for abseil.

Above and beneath were the tremendous overhangs, and poised between, gently shelving outwards at a pleasant angle, the slab continued, finishing to the left on the skyline. What lay above its limit was hidden by the overhangs. If the slab itself didn't lead to the Summit Gully then it would have to be the long overhanging crack we had seen from the First Bivouac, which was now concealed by the roofs above my head.

The only section of the route visible was the next fifty feet of the slab. From here it seemed quite holdless, but the crack I had been using for pegs where its inner edge met the overhangs continued for quite a way. Unfortunately, as far as I could make out, it seemed to end above the most blank-looking section of the slab and didn't reappear for at least ten feet. I wondered if we would have to use bolts to cross this section, but hoped we could manage without. Leaning back from the belay, I thought I could see a faint crack above the overhang just at this point. Perhaps, if we could get a peg in there, we would be able to tension left from it across the blank section of the slab. Anyway, all of this was John's problem.

Before abseiling off, I called down to him to sort out the drill and some bolts and then roped down, back to the bivouac for the brew that was on the boil. Bill and John then climbed up to my belay

John leading, and Bill at the belay on the exposed Narrow Slab. *Photo: Tony Howard*

point and John led off, prepared if necessary to spend the afternoon drilling holes in the rock. He moved up across the slab, placing the odd peg at intervals and inching slowly along, a small figure dwarfed by the colossal scale of our surroundings. He reached the impasse and, looking up from two hundred feet below, I saw him searching for cracks in the slabs. There were none. He leant out from his etriers, craning his neck to see over the roof above. Had he seen something? I couldn't contain my impatience.

'Anything there?'

His reply floated down. 'Yes, I think so; I think there's a bit of a crack high up.'

Fiddling with the pegs at his belt, he finally chose one, and then, in tension from Bill, stretched up over the roof, and despite being unable to see searched with the peg for a crack. For a few anxious moments, he prodded and probed and then suddenly, as if tired by the awkwardness of the position, he moved back to his etriers, his hand no longer holding the peg. It was in the crack.

He moved up again, this time clutching the hammer and with a few swift blows knocked the peg into position. So far, so good. He clipped in the rope and moved the etriers up for the move across the slab. If John couldn't make this with his reach, then I doubted very much if Bill or I could. He shouted down: 'Give me some tension, Bill!' Then slowly John leant down and across until he was at full stretch, almost horizontal across the slab. Held in position by the ropes from Bill, he reached out with a peg to the distant crack and drove it home. Hurriedly he clipped in an etrier, shouting, 'Slack!' Released from his position, he swung down to the peg. We were across.

John rested, and looked up, able to see for the first time what lay ahead. What would it be, the slab, or the overhanging crack? Bill and I waited silently for the answer. Both of us knew that in the next five hundred feet lay the key to the route. If there were no way out, we would be trapped. Trapped with the prospect of having to descend over two thousand feet of extremely difficult rock. But there would be a way; we were not going down. If the worst came to the worst we had enough bolts with us to drill our way up at least sixty feet of rock.

Suddenly John shouted down again, 'There's a ledge! It's about fifty feet away above the roofs.'

But there couldn't be. This was impossible. No ledge could exist in the middle of such a bristling mass of overhangs. I looked up amazed but saw nothing but bulging rock. 'Are you sure? What's above? Can you see the way out?'

'Yes, positive, and there's a groove above leading to that crack. And I think the crack's a chimney. It looks steep, but wide. With any luck it should go free.'

So that was it. We had found our way out. Hardly able to believe our good fortune I started to pack the bivouac equipment while John set off towards the ledge. Looking up I saw him disappear through a hidden groove, and then he stepped out into the heart of the overhangs. He stood up, and waved. He was on the ledge. From my position it looked impossible, a magician's illusion.

Exiting the Narrow Slab. The triangular protuberance of rock is the fourth bivouac ledge.
Photo: Tony Howard

I could hardly believe my eyes.

'How big is it?' I shouted. 'Is it large enough for a bivouac?'

The reply drifted back. 'Yes, it might just about fit us sat down, with a bit of a squeeze.'

This was a fantastic stroke of luck. We hadn't expected to find another bivouac until we reached the Summit Gully. It was, of course, without water, but fortunately we had some carrier bags with us from the grocer's shop in Åndalsnes. I filled one with snow and tied it to the sack-hauling rope to supplement our own small supply. I'd have liked to have seen the grocer's face if he'd seen one of his bags bulging with snow being pulled over the overhangs halfway up the Troll Wall.

Eager to see the ledge that John had discovered, I hurried up to Bill at my old belay and watched as he too traversed below the overhangs only to move out above them and disappear onto the ledge beyond. The sack-hauling rope hung down the overhangs, the bottom of the loop swinging in the breeze over the vertical drop below. Two grinning faces appeared above the roofs, and between them, John and Bill hauled the sacks up to their eyrie. Retreat was getting harder every day, but we were going up, not down.

I followed up across the slab, sharply aware of our magnificent situation on the edge of space. Having unclipped the carabiner and rope from the peg that had made the tension move feasible, I now found it was impossible for me to lean across. There was only one thing for it. With a tight rope from above, I pushed off from the rock and across the wall in a brief pendulum. Looking down, I delighted in the momentary vision of the screes far below. How wonderful it was to be up there on rough, dry rock beneath blue skies with no other purpose in life but to climb towards the distant summit. I moved up the groove, now just able to see Bill and John looking down, and more puzzled than ever about the mysterious ledge. As I approached, I saw with amazement that it seemed glued to the overhangs like a huge martin's nest.

I stepped onto it cautiously, half expecting the ledge to become detached from the wall. It was in a sensational position, sticking out into space like a ship's prow. Just as I reached it a helicopter flew past, breaking the silence with its clattering roar thundering and echoing from peak to peak. It returned again and again, hovering and manoeuvring near the wall. As we discovered later, our assumption that its occupants were filming the Norwegian climbers and us for Norwegian television was correct. They couldn't have picked a more spectacular moment, though we wondered if its roar would send any loose rocks tumbling down on us, or, even worse, the vibration might detach our possibly fragile perch. Finally, it made one last pass, then roared off down the valley to Åndalsnes, returning us once more to peace and solitude.

Our feelings about this brief visit were mixed. John and Bill seemed pleased about our momentary contact with the outside world, but I rather resented the intrusion. After all, half the attraction of Norway's peaks is their solitude. But, if nothing else, the helicopter provided us with a new topic for conversation as

Ole Daniel Enersen jumaring one of the hard pitches on the edge of the East Pillar above the Troll Wall. *Photo: Leif Norman Patterson.*

we sat on our small ledge. It also gave us a clue to how much the Norwegian climbers and we were becoming news, whether we wanted to or not. We also wondered if this meant the Norwegians were still on their route and how they were getting on. It must be difficult if they hadn't reached the top yet. Or maybe the helicopter was there because they were even now on the summit?

As we talked, I looked up to see what lay ahead for us. Sure enough, the overhanging crack that had puzzled us for so long was indeed a chimney. It was wet and overhanging, but obviously possible. Where there's a chimney there's usually a way. I felt sure I could see another ledge just below it and wondered if it would be larger than the one we were already on. It certainly couldn't be any smaller if the three of us were to bivvy on it.

Reluctant to leave our superb little perch I finally decided to go up the steep groove above us and have a look. Bridging up, with feet on both walls and nothing but space below, I enjoyed every inch of the exposure and the delightfully delicate climbing. On the right, the rock began to bulge outwards again into another prow. Above was the ledge, an almost exact replica of the one below, but a couple of feet longer.

I knocked in a few pegs to stop us from falling off during the night and Bill and John came up. With the sacks hung above us from the pegs, there was just enough room for the three of us to sit in comfort with our legs dangling over the edge, supported by loops of rope. We tied the stove to a peg so that it couldn't be knocked over the edge, and lifted down the carrier bag. Including the snow, there was sufficient water for some soup and a brew, and enough left after that for a brew and some porridge for breakfast in the morning. What more could we want?

As the cool chill of night crept over the wall, we hunched ourselves into the warmth of our duvets, feet swinging happily over thin air. We felt at our very best. Not even the obvious wetness of the Exit Chimney above could dampen our spirits.

Eighteen

The Fifth Day

Norwegians get there first
*'Four young Norwegians last night conquered the Trolltind Wall...
the last major north wall in Europe to be climbed. The British team was
spotted about 350ft from the summit late last night and was expected
to complete the climb today.'*

Unknown newspaper. Almost right, but we had around
1,000 feet to go when we were spotted by journalists.

UNABLE TO USE THE BIVOUAC SACKS on the cramped ledge, we spent
a chilly, restless night, waking regularly to rub cold or cramped limbs.
All of us were awake before dawn, waiting as the pale northern sky
brightened and the sun lit and warmed our faces with its long-awaited
glow. After a relaxing stretch, I balanced the stove carefully between
my body and the back of the ledge and put on the porridge for
breakfast. It thickened slowly, hissing and bubbling while we dozed
in the sunlight. Then we buried it in sugar and shared it between us,
eating it as the brew boiled and finishing with marmalade and
flatbread. Only then did we stir from our ledge and turn our thoughts
to the day's climbing. Today would decide everything.

Hardly fifty feet above, the Exit Chimney loomed outwards,
slicing a narrow gash through the last, great and otherwise

impenetrable overhangs. The leaning walls of the chimney ran black with slime draining from the Summit Gully; even the sunlight glistening on the wet rock couldn't make it look inviting. But that was the way. There was no other, and above lay the Promised Land that would lead us to the top – the Summit Gully.

John led off, belaying below the overhangs that undercut the foot of the chimney. Bill and I hoisted the sacks to him and then followed his lead. In the chimney, sparkling water dripped from the green moss clinging to its murky depths and ran down the slime-covered rock to fall at last into space or onto our upturned faces. We pulled on our cagoules as I volunteered to have a go, reaching into the wet crack with a grimace.

Surprisingly, the climbing was good. Moving suddenly over the limits of the first overhangs, the sunlit screes were revealed directly below my feet. Despite the water and slime slowly dripping over my cagoule and oozing through my trousers, I began to enjoy it. This was surprisingly good climbing. Each move was a separate problem to be solved. Having the holds covered in wet slime only made things more interesting.

I hammered in a peg or wedge at intervals for protection and moved up the ever-widening chimney, my feet bridging over the void, my left hand clutching at wet, moss-covered rock and my right jammed in the crevice, oozing black mud. The chimney curved out farther and farther over the drop and I began to feel the pitch was never-ending. Finally, and luckily, I managed to traverse out to a ledge on the dry left wall, just as John shouted there was no more rope.

For ages I hunted round for a belay but could find nothing. There were no cracks at all, so I moved down a little to a smaller ledge, really only a foothold on the lip of the overhangs, and searched again. Finally, after what felt a longer time than it took to climb the pitch, I managed to get three pegs in just over an inch or so, and tied them all together for a belay. Then I hung the pulley from them and looked at the arrangement dubiously. There was nothing to be done about it, so I shouted down, 'Right-oh, send the sacks up.'

As the first sack swung out below me into space, I cast a wary eye at the pegs, half expecting them to be ripped from the crack. But they took the strain and soon all four bags were hanging from the belay, almost surrounding me in a jumbled heap. Bill came up next and I gladly vacated my foothold for him, moving up to the comfort of the better ledge above, though still lacking a belay except for the dodgy-looking pegs Bill and the sacks were tied to.

When he was safe, or as safe as the poor pegs permitted, I led off again up the chimney, still as steep but now dry. The sidewalls no longer overhung but rose up in bulging slabs and after another full rope length they receded on the left to a sloping ledge. I stepped out onto it and found myself below the final wet, overhanging chimney. At least here at my belay it was still dry. At the top of the chimney, now temptingly near, no more than a hundred feet away, was the open entrance of the Summit Gully, spewing one half of its watery contents down our Exit Chimney, the rest going down the steep slab to my left. I belayed once again with difficulty on poor pegs and lay back on the rock to wait while John climbed up to Bill.

Down below, the white dots of Base Camp were barely visible. I wondered if the rest of the team would be able to see us through binoculars, so near to our final goal. If so, they would surely be sharing the anticipation of success that we were already feeling. And what about the Norwegians. How were they faring? If they hadn't topped out the day before, surely they would have reached the summit by now? After all, this would be their eleventh day on the wall. I guessed they would have reached the summit a couple of days ago and might perhaps, even now, be looking up at us from Base Camp.

A shout from Bill brought me back to reality as they started to haul the sacks up again. John came up immediately afterwards and moved off into the final chimney. A brief struggle and he was over the first wet roof, before striding out beyond the overhangs. I followed his progress up towards the skyline, and then suddenly he stepped left and disappeared in another conjuring trick, shouting down at the same time, 'I'm up. We're in the Summit Gully.'

Now we really began to feel the first flood of excitement. We had crossed the steepest section of the wall and the way ahead should be clear. But there was a long way to go yet and it was too early too celebrate. Bill came up to join me and once the sacks had been pulled up to John, he continued up the last chimney. I went up after him, joining them in the bottom of the gully. It looked steep but feasible, rising in gigantic steps towards a gap in the West Ridge, still concealed by the final section of the overhanging wall of Trollspiret, the pinnacle on our right. To the left, the gully wall rose at an easier angle and we thought we could see the top of the wall, the summit of Trollryggen, heaped against the sky. It didn't look far.

Aware that the afternoon was passing, I climbed off up the easy sidewall of the gully and after a full rope length, arrived on a patch of snow. I was on the very lip of the steepest section of the wall, its awe-inspiring verticality plummeting down below me for almost three thousand feet. I leant out over the drop and felt an involuntary shudder before drawing back almost immediately to the solid, reassuring comfort of the ledge. The slackening angle of the gully now looked even easier in comparison. John and Bill came up, and together we looked over the edge, suddenly very aware of the drop we had been climbing over for the last few days. Before, we had been immersed in it but now we were safely above, we felt its pull.

Confident there was no one down below, we threw a stone out into space. It seemed to fall forever. We watched it silently, unable to tear our eyes from the tiny speck plunging downwards. And still it fell, and we leant out even further trying to estimate where it would land on the screes. But it didn't land. It kept on falling. When it seemed it should have hit the screes, it simply disappeared from sight below the outline of the wall – and still it fell. We stayed motionless on the edge of the drop, gripped in fascination, watching, waiting, listening and eventually, long after it seemed to have been swallowed up in the bowels of the earth, the dreadful booming crash of it hitting the screes rose up into the still air. We pulled ourselves back onto the ledge and sat down clutching our belay for security.

It was six o'clock. Unknown to us, the Norwegians were just reaching the summit. As they said later, if they had known how near we were to the top, they would have waited and bivouacked there to meet us. But they didn't know; they hadn't seen us since we had first started the climb five days ago. They rested in the evening sun that even now was lighting the summit wall so provocatively above us and then started on the descent.

Meanwhile, we wondered about bivouacking on our ledge and making for the top in one long dash the next day. After all, it didn't look too hard, but summit gullies never do. As we knew from experience, most of them have a sting in the tail. And anyway, the urge to head for the top now was taking over. We decided to eat what little bulky food remained then throw the sack-hauling rope over the edge and carry the sacks up the remainder of the route. Apart from having eaten most of our food, we had used around half our pegs and the difference in weight was considerable. It would mean a great saving in time and the prospect encouraged us. Happy with our plan, we sat back and enjoyed our evening meal as the spear-like shadows of the trolls once more stretched themselves over the valley.

Disturbed by an unexpected shout, we looked around amazed, searching for the owner of the voice still echoing between the peaks. Apart from our own, it was the first human voice we had heard for five days. Our isolation had been broken. Bill spotted them first, a group of climbers in a gap below the peak of Store Trolltind almost immediately opposite. We felt sure that they must be from the press, as we had heard rumours before starting the climb that they were going up there for photographs. We shouted back and waved and this time we were all three glad of the intrusion. Somehow we felt that they were able to share our feeling of achievement in reaching the Summit Gully. They would take the news to the valley and to Base, and Mag and the lads would know we were on our way to the top. They waved again before they started on their descent, disappearing behind the towering trolls that overlooked the wall.

The urge to reach the top and get back down to Base, to its comforts and to Mag's delicious, enormous meals was irresistible. We packed hurriedly, trying to spread the weight as evenly as possible into three sacks. Then, as a final symbolic gesture that the wall was defeated, we coiled up the sack-hauling rope and hurled it over the edge. Its ends flailed wildly in the rush of wind as it fell silently through over half a mile of air. With a last downward glance I shouldered my still cumbersome sack and set off into the gully.

The climbing was straightforward and with deliberate, balanced movements the sacks were not too much of a hindrance. But it was getting colder and as Bill followed behind me I looked up at the skies overhead. Thin strands of cloud were beginning to drift round the summit spires and reach tentatively towards the gully. Surely the weather wasn't going to break now, when the climb was so nearly in our grasp? For a few moments a light drizzle fell and then stopped; it hardly wet the rocks, but it was a warning. In bad weather the gully could become a torrent and we still had almost a thousand feet to go.

We started hurrying, caught irresistibly in our desire to reach the top and amazing ourselves with the speed of our movement now there were no sacks to haul. Questions ran through my mind. Perhaps we would make it tonight? Perhaps the gully would be easy? I doubted it. I have always been cautious about that kind of situation. Better to hope for the best and plan for the worst. That way I save myself from disappointment yet still get the most pleasure if the best happens.

We climbed on up the gully, now forced into its confines, occasionally filled with hard frozen snow or dripping ice. A cool wind began to blow upwards between the damp walls. Wisps of cloud above us drifted uncertainly before tearing into shreds and disappearing in the night sky. Once again the trolls stood aloof above us and a solitary star appeared as the air cleared above the gully's mouth.

With a couple of hours to go before midnight we reached an impasse as the gully ended abruptly at two vertical walls of rock forming a corner split by a thin, tough-looking crack. The only escape lay up a wider crack in the left wall, guarded by overhangs at a hundred feet. Here it was: the sting in the tail. Tiring a little, John took the lead and climbed up to a small stance some thirty feet below the roof. Apart from our rest at the foot of the gully, we had been climbing for sixteen hours on this fifth day. Bill moved up to the belay, leaving me with no room to join them on the ledge. Not feeling at all keen, I led past them towards the small roof, determined to crack what I hoped would be the last problem.

Now on steep rock, my sack, which still weighed over fifty pounds began to drag at my shoulders, pulling me down as I moved with sluggish deliberation to the overhang. I reached up, jamming my fingers into the crack that split the roof and braced my legs across the walls of the corner. It was useless. My fingers ached and my sack was pulling me backwards. With grim memories of climbing with my sack on the Great Wall, I dropped back down to the recess below. I rested my head on the cool rock, my arms hanging limply at my sides, hands clenching and unclenching in an effort to ease some strength back into them.

'It's no good,' I shouted down. 'I'll have to leave my sack here.' I took a peg from my belt and drove it into a crack, slipping the leaden weight of the pack from my shoulders and clipping it to the carabiner.

Moving up again, I now felt light and capable of continuing. Pulling over the overhang, I struggled desperately to raise my feet higher but there was nothing. I slid back to the peg unable to hold myself any longer. It was midnight. The damp chill of the rock was freezing my fingers while sweat ran out from under my helmet. I swore at the rock, calling the crack every name I could think of and hunting for a channel peg to hammer into its depths. But all I had were two thin horizontal pegs clipped forlornly to my belt.

Placing these as high as I could in a crack on the right, I hung slings from them and pulled up until I was stood in the slings and my back was jammed on the opposite wall above the overhang. I reached up, searching again for the crack until my fingers found it. I jammed them in and with a heave took my feet from the slings and struggled up into the groove. Too late I discovered there were no holds and my feet scrabbled uselessly at the rock. I was coming off.

Feverishly, I searched amongst the slings round my neck with cold, fumbling fingers and found one with a small nut threaded on it. I yanked it over my head and flicked it at arm's length up into the crack. The nut jammed first time and I swung from the loop as my feet skated away from the rock. Sweating and cursing, I pulled up on the sling and climbed past it to a small ledge. Fifty feet above was a larger ledge with snow and hardly three hundred feet away was the top of the gully – the top of the wall. 'Okay,' I yelled, 'I'm up. There's a bivvy just above and I can see the top.'

Bill came up next, fighting his way over the overhang and between us we pulled the sacks up on the climbing rope. John followed and by two in the morning, twenty hours after leaving our perch above the Narrow Slab, we had reached the bivouac. The top of the wall beckoned invitingly only a couple of rope lengths away. Barring a disaster, the route was in the bag but by now we were too tired to care. It would all be more fun in the morning. We unpacked for our last night and, in clothing still wet from the Exit Chimney, crawled into the bivouac sacks for the last time.

Only then did we realise we could now see the lights of Åndalsnes, shining beyond the hills to the north with a yellow, glowing friendliness. How welcome they were, and how near they seemed, and yet, how strange to think that tomorrow, all being well, we would be back down there in a different world with the rest of the team.

But that was tomorrow. Tonight a cold, insistent wind was blowing up the gully and clouds were forming thickly out over the fjords beyond Åndalsnes. The wind was changing. The mists were returning to the trolls, concealing their looming presence in swirling eddies of cloud before sinking down into the gully, wrapping us too in their damp embrace, only to be swept away again by the blustering wind. But above the mouth of the gully, the solitary star still shone, keeping us company until dawn.

Nineteen

The Sixth Day: Success

This fierce urge to conquer

'The three British climbers in their red anoraks, clinging to each other on the 6,000 foot summit of the Trolltind Wall in Norway could scarcely help having a sense of history. They had just made the epic first ascent of the mountain, an awesome climb with a face a mile high. It was to the day the hundredth anniversary of Edward Whymper's conquest of the Matterhorn.'

Dermot Purgavie, Daily Sketch. It wasn't the first ascent of the mountain, and the centenary of the first ascent of the Matterhorn was nine days earlier on 14 July.

WE SPENT THE NEXT THREE HOURS huddled together, shivering in the bivvy bag. It was numbingly cold and the night seemed interminable. We dozed only at intervals, curled against each other for warmth we couldn't find, watching clouds creep and twist around us. After five days of climbing in almost perpetual shade we resigned ourselves to reaching the summit in cloud and being robbed of the sunshine, warmth and view that should be ours.

At five o'clock, the mists took on a brighter shade as the sun slid over the horizon. As we cooked our last breakfast, they began to thin, dissolving and disappearing to reveal the trolls looking down on us from the lip of the wall. Down below, the valleys were cloaked by a thick sea of cloud that had rolled in overnight, but even that began to lift and break.

Gulping down a steaming pan of tea, we repacked the sodden bivouac sacks. I traversed back into the gully, now filled with a steep snow slope that ended below the final wall. Hidden by the walls of the gully, we were still in the shadow, unable to reap the benefit of the sunlight that was already dazzling the trolls. We longed for the moment we would step off this shadowed, vertical half-world into a world of sunlight and unimpeded views to every horizon, not just the one at our backs.

I cut steps up the snow slope and belayed below the last vertical wall of rock where the gully narrowed to a massive chimney. It was blocked by a huge boulder, but I could see a narrow crack up the back. Could this be our escape?

John climbed up to me, his hands numbed by contact with the snow, and peered up towards the hole. It would obviously not be possible wearing a sack so he left his with me before setting off. I saw his arms disappear, then his head and then, with one last jerk, his legs followed through the gap and he was soon looking down from the top of the chimney. Once Bill had joined me, I followed and we pulled the sacks up the outside of the boulder. Bill came up next, appearing with a grin from the hole, then leading off up the steep slab above. He reached a belay below a small overhang. Sunlight was baking the wall, just a few feet above his head. John and I craned our necks. Surely he must be near the top now? But we hadn't time to ask before he shouted down, 'We're there! I'm level with the gap in the ridge. It's just a few feet to the right, past an overhang.'

'Not another bloody overhang,' I thought. 'Do they never end?' Then, aloud, 'How's it look? Will it go free?'

'Yeah. Piece of cake. There looks to be good handholds all over it. Come on up.'

I didn't need to be asked twice and leapt at the slab, which proved deceptively delicate, to join Bill. Just a few feet away was the sunlight, streaming through the gap. John followed quickly and led through for the final pitch. He reached out across the final overhang, grasped a large, friendly jug and swung over. A few more moves and he was up. Dropping his sack, he belayed for the last time and took in the ropes. The sunlight caught his grinning face while Bill and I remained crouched below the final overhang in shadow until the long length of rope was taken in and I too could swing out from the stance. One last look below, one final move on vertical rock and suddenly it was over. A whole new world was at my feet.

Quickly we took the last length of rope in and Bill heaved himself up to join us. We tore off our sacks and our wet duvets, untied the ropes and ran into the sun, laughing and congratulating each other. We basked in its heat; we revelled in the unfamiliar, almost horizontal surroundings. Collapsing in a tired heap on the rough, warm rocks, we drank in the unsurpassable beauty of the view, relaxing as the tensions of the last few days drained from our minds and muscles, leaving us limp and contented. No more striving upwards. No more anything.

Gone was the sombre, shadowed isolation of the wall. Instead, the world was warm, and full of life and colour. On the far horizon, previously hidden snow-capped peaks glittered like diamonds in the sunlight. Nearer, rising up from the unseen depths of Isterdal, soaring blue-grey walls of glaciated rock curved up gracefully to form a trio of dramatic summits, Bispen, Kongen and Dronninga. Beneath us, deep blue tarns nestled in lonely snow-filled cwms and on the screes a ptarmigan, disturbed by our presence, flew up, breaking the silence with its croak. From between the crevices in the grey, quartz-streaked rock, tiny Alpine flowers bobbed their pink heads and everywhere the rock was tinted with dry crusts of red, orange and yellow lichen. How good it would have been to lie there idly all day while the sun curved lazily through the sky, but we had yet to reach the summit and a few puffs of cloud were still skimming across the horizon.

After a delightfully lazy hour we reluctantly picked up our sacks and scrambled up the last few hundred feet of the West Ridge to the top before relaxing again in the sunshine. We wondered if they would be able to see us from Base and on the off chance that someone might be looking we took out the red bivouac sacks and waved to them. Down at Base nothing happened for a moment then suddenly we saw an answering wave of something dark against the white dot of a tent. Miraculously, they had seen us. They knew we were up. Sharing their undoubted relief and excitement, we laughed and shouted even though we knew they couldn't hear us. Overcome by the realisation of our success and the effort of the last few days, we sat down again in the sunshine. We were definitely on top of the world.

As we cooked some porridge and made a brew with the summit snow, we wondered what would be happening down at Base. Little did we know that everyone was there: Mag, Rob, Jeff, and Nick of course, but also the Norwegian team and their two girlfriends, the press, the Norwegian State Radio crew and countless others. Already they were leaving for their cars to bring Mag and the lads up the valley of Isterdal to meet us.

Meanwhile, we sat contentedly in the sunshine and only when the clouds on the distant horizon began to creep nearer like grey wolves surrounding their prey did we take heed and stir ourselves to begin the long descent. Our bodies, no longer spurred on by the need for action, were lethargic and unwilling. In the unfamiliar blazing heat of the afternoon we slithered down dazzling slopes of soft snow, our eyes straining against the whiteness. The sacks hung heavily on our shoulders but a burden had been lifted from our minds. Trudging wearily through the heavy snow, we looked back at the jagged summit with pride. It was ours. The trolls stood on the top like old friends – they had let us win and had shared their most closely guarded secrets.

Yet the descent seemed endless, down long, silent, lonely valleys of snow, on past green-blue pools of melting ice, past unclimbed purple-shadowed cliffs, down, down into a world of grey scree, fresh green bracken and rushing streams. The streams grew larger, fed from the high rocky gullies and the melting snows. Merging to form torrents, they gurgled beneath stretches of snow before escaping to leap over boulders. At the valley's rim, they cascaded in one wild roaring plunge down a thousand feet of slabs into Isterdal, joining the water from the even more powerful waterfall of Stigfoss, which drowned the hairpin road in its spray.

On the viewpoint above Stigfoss, a group of figures stood waiting. As we climbed slowly down through the heather and bracken, they started running towards us. It was the rest of our team. Our dusty faces broke into grins, our legs, tired and aching from the descent gained new life as we hurried towards them. They took our sacks, besieging us with questions, intoxicating us with congratulations.

Norwegian and British teams at the celebratory dinner, Grand Hotel Åndalsnes. Left to right, top row – Margaret Woodcock, Jon Teigland, Leif Norman Patterson, John Amatt, Tony Howard, Rob Holt, Odd Eliassen, Helene Olsen, Ole Daniel Enersen. Left to right, front row – Jeff Heath, Bill Tweedale, Rotraut Hofmann and Tony 'Nick' Nicholls. *Photo: Margaret Woodcock Collection*

At the roadside, bottles of cool, sparkling lager were thrust into our hands. We drank long and deep until liquid spilled over our laughing faces. Everyone was talking at once. The Norwegians had sent their congratulations having reached the top the previous night. They were waiting for us at the Grand Hotel in Åndalsnes. Both teams were invited to a celebration dinner that night in honour of the event. Right then, the Rolling Stones were getting 'no satisfaction', but we certainly got ours.

We were whisked away in a car as cameras clicked and the grey clouds gathered solemnly on the peaks. Down we went, round countless hairpins, beneath the roaring falls and darkening, ominous skies. As we arrived in Åndalsnes lightning lit the rolling clouds, the lonely trolls silhouetted against the flash. Thunder echoed over the mountains, and as we dashed into the hotel, the storm began. The Norwegians ran to meet us and the handshakes and congratulations were mutual and genuine. We talked happily as course after course of delicious food arrived while outside the wind and rain lashed at the windows and the wall of the trolls ran black with water.

The following night, both parties were again guests at the Grand Hotel where we were all presented with inscribed champagne buckets and miniatures of Norwegian Pewter known as 'Troll Tin'. The inscription read: 'First ascent Trollveggen 1965' with the names of the members of both expeditions beneath. The presentation was made on behalf of the Norwegian Travel Association of Åndalsnes in recognition of the publicity our climbs had brought to the area.

At the speech following the dinner, Leif Norman Patterson said how pleased he was that the two expeditions from different countries should have been able to climb and help each other without jealousy or competition, with which we were happy to concur.

During the following week the Norwegians removed most of their fixed rope from the wall. Rob, Jeff and Nick offered to collect ours, which was hugely appreciated, climbing up as far as The Nick in atrocious weather and removing all but one short length of rope. John, Bill and myself took the easy option and retrieved the last tent from Advance, now ripped to shreds by falling boulders.

On the last day of July we said goodbye to our newfound friends in Åndalsnes. John suddenly had to return home, but the rest of us sailed north for the second half of our summer holiday, escaping from the press, enjoying more mountain exploration and meeting old friends in the Arctic islands of Vesteralen. Returning to Reka, which I had climbed in 1962, Nick, Bill, Rob and Jeff made the first ascent of its South East Face up a 1,300-foot diédre, with numerous hard pitches. Maggie and I met them on top after climbing the South West Ridge. The whole team also topped out on nearby previously unclimbed summits.

Returning home a month later we were fêted by our local council, which a few months earlier had been reluctant to help with sponsorship. I was also faced with requests for lectures and magazine articles, which John was already well into following his earlier return. Bob Brigham of Ellis Brigham Mountain Sports knew us all personally and had been a main sponsor. He treated us all to a slap-up meal in Manchester. It seemed that, unexpectedly, our summer holiday had turned us all into heroes.

PART SIX

Afterwards

TWENTY

A Lifetime Ago

There's a race of men that don't fit in,
A race that can't stay still;
So they break the hearts of kith and kin,
And they roam the world at will.
They range the field and they rove the flood,
And they climb the mountain's crest;
Theirs is the curse of the gypsy blood,
And they don't know how to rest.
Robert Service

THERE WAS SOMETHING SPECIAL ABOUT THE RIMMON ROUTE. It wasn't just a first on the wall, it was a first for us as climbers too. You never repeat an experience like that. But Romsdal had got under my skin. At Christmas 1966, after three hard months of exciting adventures earning money on Icelandic trawlers and a Danish cargo boat with other lads from the Rimmon, I arrived back in Norway. With me was Wayne Gartside, a young toughie from Oldham known to everyone as 'Owdham Roughyed'. Wayne was a recent Rimmon Club recruit. When we signed on the cargo boat, we hadn't known that Norway was the ship's ultimate destination. There was no plan. The only plan I had was to get away from England and the continuing fuss about the Troll Wall, but being in Norway the pull of Romsdal was too much. Rob and Jeff had been on the trawlers with us and Rob soon turned up to join the fun. Bill followed soon after, along with Smiler, my partner on the recce, and some other Rimmon lads including Brian Hodgkinson, who had been on the first British ascent of Kongen's East Face in 1963. It turned into quite a scene.

Roy Brown, an ex-Manchester Gritstone lad and one of my earliest climbing friends also came out. He had been working as an instructor for the Mountaineering Association in North Wales and Austria, and I had been instructing at Plas y Brenin and the Outward Bound and had just received my BMC Guide's certificate. Together with Rob, Bill and Keith Chadwick, another Rimmon lad with whom I had done some good routes in the Dolomites, we started guiding in Romsdal, spending around six months a year there for the next three years, guiding, odd-jobbing, repeating the classic climbs and adding numerous new routes on previously unclimbed valley crags as well as on long outstanding problems including two of Romsdal's three great pillars.

The Pillars rise from close to sea level to almost 6,000 feet. The East Pillar of Trollryggen bounding the left edge of the Troll Wall had been climbed by Ralph Høibakk and Arne Randers Heene in 1958 and had had few subsequent ascents. Per Harvold, a friend of ours from Åndalsnes, had tried it and even crashed a small plane trying to get a closer look. He asked Bill and me if we would like to guide him up it. We jumped at the chance and had a great two days on the climb with Per, the three of us finding our way unerringly through the complexities of the overlapping slabs that make up the lower half of the pillar and enjoying our bivvy on the edge of the Troll Wall. Our growing familiarity with Romsdal rock was obviously paying dividends.

The other two pillars were obvious targets. Bill and I made the first ascent of the East Pillar of Breitind, making good time and topping out in a day, as we did on the East Pillar of Semletind

Bill belaying on the first ascent of the East Pillar of Semletind, Romsdal. *Photo: Tony Howard*

(previously known as Søndre Trolltind), where we were joined by Rob and Wayne, climbing in two separate ropes, though the route turned into an epic when we were caught in a blizzard and violent thunderstorm a thousand feet from the top. A lightning strike on the summit caused a rockfall, one rock hitting Bill on the head. His helmet was split, and blood poured down his ashen face, as he swung limply and silently from the rope. We thought he was dead but he soon perked up, refusing an offer to bivvy and have a brew, and following valiantly on a tight rope up the wall into the white-out. We got lost but eventually found a bivouac boulder we knew and spent the night under it.

John also turned up for a few weeks in 1967, making the first ascent of the North Face of Semletind with Rusty Baillie over a six-day period, before emigrating to Canada. It was good to see them both. I hadn't seen Rusty since we were both instructing at Plas y Brenin in 1962, climbing together in North Wales, the Peak and the Lakes. Their route in Romsdal was a real plum, taking a direct line up the centre of the last of the valley's unclimbed north faces. It seemed everyone was there over the coming years, with new routes being done everywhere.

Pete Livesey and John Stanger were among the first, making the second ascent of the Rimmon Route. Lots of big names stopped by, including Joe Brown and Tom Patey, Doug Scott, Jim Duff, Tony Wilmott, Ed Drummond, Ben Campbell-Kelly as well as climbers from around Europe, all wanting to make their mark on the Troll Wall and other big faces in the area. John Stanger returned to make two hard big-wall routes on the previously unclimbed Mongejura at the head of the valley, both around 3,500 feet. He also beat us to one of the area's 'last great problems', the 4,500-foot East Face of Kongen, the crux of which is a seventy-foot roof crossed by a hundred feet of aid climbing with a stance in etriers to finish.

John, Brian Thompson, Dave Walsh and Jon Teigland, one of the Norwegian Troll Wall team, climbed the route in 1967. Rob, Bill,

Wayne and myself had tried it that spring, too early in the season, bivouacking a couple of pitches below the roof, which is over halfway up the face. As the sun rose and we started out next morning, the summit snows began to melt. Drips of water falling from the lip of the roof soon became a torrential waterfall. It was unclimbable.

Soaked, we retreated and escaped left, bivouacking again in a rock basin under the upper South East Face, before moving back in above the roof and summiting after another bivouac, once again in atrocious blizzard and white-out conditions. Luckily for us, we were met on the top on our fourth day by Halvor Sødahl, a photographer friend from Åndalsnes and other local climbers, including one of Romsdal's pioneers, Herbert Grüner with his son Torleif.

Almost thirty years previously, Herbert had been involved in a terrible accident when trying to make the first ascent of the East Face of Kongen's neighbour, Dronninga – The Queen – in the autumn of 1939. Over halfway up the 4,500-foot face, the leader of their group of three, Henrik Oshaug, had run out of rope.

White-out on the summit of Kongen. Left to right: Wayne Gartside, Tony Howard, Bill Tweedale and Rob Holt. *Photo: Halvor Sødahl*

Herbert, who was then twenty three, untied from the middle of their seventy-foot line so Henrik could continue. Herbert and the third man, Johan Bolsø, held the rope, but had nothing to belay on. A little higher up, Henrik fell, taking with him Johan, who was still tied on, and leaving Herbert alone but without a rope.

Unable to reverse the route, Herbert eventually managed to reach a safe place in which he could wedge himself to spend the night, but only after removing his shoes to climb a thin crack with his toes. Having filled his sack with grass to keep himself warm, he survived the night without any water, and eventually attracted the attention of rescuers in the valley by shouting and burning pieces from his shirt and a tobacco box so they could see where he was. His rescuers, finally arrived within thirty feet of him but were unable to climb nearer, so Herbert used his shoelaces and thread from his socks to make a line, which he weighted with a small stone to lower down to them, so that he could haul up a thin line to which the rope was attached. He was rescued after twenty six hours alone on the wall. Such were the hazards of climbing in those early days. A couple of years later Herbert was arrested by the Nazis for being in the resistance, and sent to a prison camp from where he eventually managed to get a letter home to say, 'It's okay here, but it was better on Dronninga!'

Romsdal's valley crags provided us with climbing opportunities when the big walls were out of condition. They were usually a much less serious alternative and offered everything from a single pitch to thousand-foot routes. None had been climbed on and if the weather was good we would pop out at all times of day and night, sometimes after watching a film at the local 'Kino' or after a party or village barn dance where the band was usually the Horgheim Trio, known to us as the Orgasm Trio. These dances were great fun, though we were really into other music, which was coming over from the States. It was 'The Summer of Love' and the hippie revolution was in full swing. In California the Monterey

Festival had brought together Jefferson Airplane, The Who, Jimi Hendrix and Janis Joplin. Romsdal was rocking.

It was all great fun. Luckily for me, Alan Waterhouse, my partner in our new company Troll, despite having a day job to support his family, managed to carry on without me, manufacturing and selling our new designs of Troll nuts and waist-belts while I enjoyed myself climbing and guiding in Norway. Back home from Romsdal for the winter months I took over the daily work of running Troll while at weekends we all carried on exploring the valleys of Derbyshire for the forthcoming *Northern Limestone* guidebook.

By 1970, we had all moved on from Romsdal. The Rimmon began to break up as a lot of the lads either settled down or moved abroad. Nick, who had been unable to join us in the intervening years because of work had joined another climbing club, the Black and Tans, choosing to concentrate on climbing in the UK. Rob and Bill were also busy at work in England. All three were still climbing hard, though all now had family responsibilities, which meant fewer long trips. Even so, Bill still managed to get to Greenland with me a couple of years later, before working mostly abroad, erecting heavy machinery.

Rob, as he put it, became 'a traveller in Scandinavian ladies' clothing'. As nice a picture as that paints, he was in fact delivering ladies' clothing to Scandinavia. He later set up his own haulage business, trucking all over Europe and as far as Turkey, eventually selling up and becoming a transport manager for a big company before retiring. Though he climbed less over the years he is still out on the hills walking and enjoying the mountain scene, as is Maggie, who married Bill Birch, a climber from the Black and Tans. When I spoke to her while preparing this book, she had just completed the 258-mile Cornish Coastal Path.

Jeff Heath continued his nomadic ways. After being with us on the Icelandic trawlers, he did some instructing at the Devon Outward Bound, getting married a couple of years later. The police found him naked in the street on his stag night. Soon after that he left for Australia with his wife, Sandy, where he worked as a teacher. Not long ago, he emailed to say he had been 'doing some good things with his students in Outdoor Education: bushwalking, camping, orienteering, canoeing and even a bit of climbing before all the adventure is regulated and certificated out of life.' He lives 'on a ten-acre plot that we share with fourteen sheep, at least three possums, dozens of birds, one cat and on occasion fifteen to twenty kangaroos'. Having retired, he took up sailing, which has become a major passion. Forty five years on, he still vanishes for long periods, and at the time of writing is believed to be 'somewhere in the North West Territories'.

For John and myself it was different. Unexpectedly the ascent of the Troll Wall was to play a massive part in both of our lives. John emigrated to Canada in 1968, initially as a teacher but, following on from the Troll Wall climb and his subsequent route on Semletind, he rapidly carved out a very impressive career for himself as a motivational speaker and mountaineer, leading expeditions to remote regions of northern Norway, Peru, Nepal, China and Greenland with six Arctic visits, making many first ascents of previously unclimbed peaks. In 1981, his expedition to Western China made a lightweight ascent of Muztagh Ata, the highest peak in the world to have been ascended and descended entirely on skis. John also organised and participated in Canada's first successful Everest expedition. Qualified as a Canadian Mountain Guide, he organised the first Banff Mountain Film Festival, now a well-known annual event.

I also ended up in Canada for a couple of years. Now married to a Norwegian girl and with a daughter, I needed to earn some money. Selling Troll nuts and waist-belts in 1970 didn't feed a family. With our prototype Whillans Harness now being tested by Don for the Annapurna South Face Expedition, I headed for the Yukon, a part of the world that had always attracted me. Landing in New York with just enough money for a bus ticket to Canada, I finally arrived penniless on the Trans-Canada Highway. Sleeping in a snowdrift in temperatures way below zero at the side of the road in my sleeping bag, I was woken at dawn by the sound of a horn and hissing airbrakes. I had a lift, and what a lift, all the way across the country to Edmonton.

The driver offered me a bed in a motel room the first night, which I refused saying I would kip in the cab if that was okay, but he wouldn't have it, so I joined him for a meal, also at his expense, and then discovered there was only one bed, a double. He wouldn't listen to any talk of sleeping on the floor, so I climbed warily in with him. He cracked a couple of beers, turned on the TV and slotted some coins into the bed, which to my surprise began rocking. Things were turning strange.

My concerns were unfounded; he was a great guy, a French Canadian and grandson of one of the Hudson Bay Company *voyageurs* who used to travel the country by canoe, trading and collecting furs. I travelled with him for a week, helping to offload his truck at stops along the way, eating and sleeping with him and being paid at the end of the journey. It was a good start. In Edmonton I got a doss at the Salvation Army hostel and a week later had found myself a job in an opencast mine in the Yukon. Six weeks later I had enough money to bring my wife and daughter over. With both of us working, we were earning around £400 a week instead of the twenty quid I was getting back home.

Two years later, we had enough money in the bank to buy a house with plenty left over and a thousand-mile canoe trip under my belt, along an old Klondike gold rush route from Canada's North West Territories to the Yukon and Alaska. I swapped the canoe for a VW Beetle, which I had to dig out from beneath a snowdrift, and the three of us set off for home on what became a six-month trip. We travelled down the west coast of Canada, seeing The Stones in Vancouver, then on through the USA to Yosemite, where I did a couple of routes on Royal Arches and Cathedral. From there we continued over Tuolumne to Death Valley and on past the Grand Canyon – all the way to Panama. There my wife and daughter caught a boat home and I worked my passage back on a Norwegian cargo boat. It seems old habits die hard.

Once at sea I met the skipper for the first time. 'I didn't know you were a hippie,' he said, eyeing my shoulder-length hair with distaste. 'Get up the mast and wash it,' he added grumpily, obviously thinking this was some sort of punishment. What fun. I spent half a day up there high above the ship, swinging around and scrubbing away at the salt, enjoying the fresh sea air. In the end I was told to come down and wash the bridge floor around the captain's feet, which I did with great gusto, before being banished from his sight for the rest of the trip, to paint some rusting bulkheads. I didn't care. I was not only on a freebie home but earning money.

Back at Troll, there were now three of us: myself, Alan Waterhouse and Paul Seddon, who had been manufacturing his own range of nuts under the name of Parba. He had joined Troll when I left for Canada, making it a more viable proposition. The Whillans Harness was taking over from the Mark 2 and held centre-stage worldwide until 1979 when rumours that Wild Country were designing a harness forced a re-think.

By then I was the designer at Troll and started off by playing around with our Mark 2 waist-belt, the one we had used on the Troll Wall. It could be attached to a sit sling to make a crude sit harness, a bit like the American Forrest Harness that was also made at Troll. My objective was to combine the separate waist and leg loops into a one-piece sit harness. It wasn't working. The sitting position was uncomfortable, whereas the Whillans, despite rumours to the contrary, was very comfortable.

Why did the Whillans work? I climbed in it all the time and frequently had hanging belays, but to check, I hung in it from our harness testing beam in the mill, to remind myself what was going on. The answer was immediately obvious. It worked because the crutch strap we had designed with Don for the Annapurna climb took the load first, moving up and away from the body, and lifting the leg loops before sharing the load with the waist belt.

This took a smaller proportion of the weight, the bulk of the load being round the thighs. The problem was simple. How could I repeat that without copying the Whillans crutch design?

Sitting in the Whillans, suspended from the beam, I had one of those 'Eureka!' moments: a small loop would do exactly what the upper half of the Whillans crutch did. All it needed was a different shape of leg loops to go with it. The Troll machinists, who could stitch anything from nylon webbing, quickly made the first sample. Then, together with my partners, Alan and Paul, we tweaked it a bit and it worked. The world's first 'belay loop' harness was born. Within a year it was copied by the world's harness manufacturers and rapidly became the template for almost all climbing harnesses, even today. Equally groundbreaking were our sewn tape slings, which were treated with great suspicion at the time, so much so that we had to use two sets of sewing instead of one. So familiar and ubiquitous are both these developments, it seems odd to think both have been around for only thirty years.

Alan, Paul and I continued to work together at Troll until we got a good offer for the company in 1995, thirty years after Alan and I had started it. It was time to move on. We had become Britain's leading harness designers and manufacturers and had a wide range of other climbing and industrial safety gear to complement it, all originating with the Mark 2 waist-belt and nuts used on the Troll Wall in 1965. The camaraderie of the early years was going. As far as I was concerned, it was becoming a commercial rat race, more about making money than making climbing gear. Gone were the days when Troll made web gear, Denny Moorhouse of Clog made metal gear, Pete Hutchinson and Pete Merron of Mountain Equipment made down gear and we all kipped on the floor at Denny's mum's house for the Harrogate Trade Show. Gone were the days when product innovation was a company's life-blood.

By the 1990s it was all about expansion and competition. Every company made or sold every product. Fashion and colour were often more important than product design. Business was simply about profit margins and growth and keeping the accountants and bank manager happy. New Health and Safety regulations inhibited innovation. Sitting in interminable meetings I found my mind wandering the hills and dreaming of my next trip rather than concentrating on boring figures. Designing and making climbing gear had always been my motivation for working at Troll. Money was secondary. It was time to get out, away from balance sheets and back to the real world of rock and wild places.

Not that I ever left it. During the years at Troll after 1972 when I returned from Canada, I had at least one big trip every year. The first was with Bill Tweedale and a team of Danish climbers lead by Dolfi Rotovnik to East Greenland. Our objective was the first ascent of Ingolffjeld's 6,000-foot East Face, but it didn't go well. Bill and I were involved in a monster rockfall as a huge tower fell from the summit 3,000 feet above us and careered down the face, crashing in pieces all around our bivouac, covering us in dust and filling the air with the smell of cordite. I have no idea how we weren't killed, but we emerged miraculously unscathed only to watch the debris continue down the wall and out across the glacier for a few hundred yards almost to Base Camp. Then a few rope lengths higher at the next bivvy, the bad weather came in and we were forced to retreat as snow settled ever deeper. Nevertheless, just before leaving for the walk-out, we made a nice one-day ascent of a nearby summit we named the Angdan Tower while the rest of the team explored some previously unvisited peaks across the valley.

These annual trips continued through all my years at Troll. By now, Bill, like other members of the old Troll Wall team, was tied up with family. His work as an engineer took him abroad for much of the time so he was rarely able to climb. As a result, having been invited once more by the Danes, I returned to Greenland the following year with my regular climbing partner Mick Shaw, climbing one of a beautiful group of pillars, these days known to climbers as the Fox Jaw Towers. We also climbed in The Hoggar in Algeria's Sahara desert, and in Iran. We got ourselves thrown out of the Karun Canyon, supposed location of a 6,000-foot cliff, in the Zagros Mountains by the Iranian army. But we did find and make the first ascent of the 3,000-foot limestone wall of Kuh-e-Bisotun in Iranian Kurdistan.

Like many climbers, I made frequent trips to the Alps and Dolomites. I also climbed in the Picos with Adrian Garlick, making what we were told was the first British ascent of the delightful Rabada-Navarro route on Naranjo de Bulnes. Attending trade fairs in Europe for Troll, I'd always find time to climb in places like the Pfalz and Donautal with Di Taylor, one of the original Rimmon members, who now worked with me at Troll on the design side. In later years, with both our marriages over, Di joined Mick and I on our annual desert-mountain trips, climbing on the domes of Kassala in eastern Sudan and trekking across Jebel Marra in the west, in Darfur. As always, despite their abject poverty, the village people gave us every possible welcome. It's terrible to think what destruction has been brought to their villages and lives in recent years by the government-backed Janjaweed fighters.

Morocco was always a favourite. I first went there in the winter of 1963 on an early Rimmon trip, climbing Toubkal, North Africa's highest summit, and discovering the climbing area of Tafraoute. I'd loved my time in Morocco, both the climbing and the people, and leapt at the chance to return in 1979, heading south for some warm sun and becoming the first Brits to climb in Morocco's Taghia Canyon. It was there we met French guides Wilf Colonna and Bernard Domenech who, in later years, we invited to join us on our sponsored exploratory trips to Wadi Rum and Oman. On this same trip we made an early descent of the M'Goun Gorge, together with Mick's girlfriend, my daughter and Di Taylor and her eldest son. Also in Morocco, at the request of the Royal Society for the Protection of Birds and the Moroccan National Parks, we worked together on a dangerously loose and overhanging sea cliff, to create new nesting ledges for the critically endangered Northern Bald Ibis, putting model birds in place to attract the Ibis and thereby aid their recovery. Only sixty pairs of this species remained in the wild.

Mick and I also had trips to Norway, climbing again in Romsdal and in south Norway where we discovered nice climbing near the coast and on the 1,000-foot sweep of the Setesdal Slabs. By the late 1990s there were a dozen routes on the Troll Wall, but ours was the big classic and still the most popular. As we recognised on our winter recce, it was the easiest line on the face, and as such was inescapable, but it was no pushover; the only way off was up or down the route, with all the problems that could entail. And it passed through some stunning and formidable rock architecture, in particular The Nick, The Great Wall, and the spectacularly exposed Narrow Slab. All the while the potentially insuperable obstacle of the frequently wet overhanging Exit Chimney loomed above, keeping a successful outcome in doubt almost to the end, as a good route should.

Mick Shaw exploring new crags near Setesdal in southern Norway, in the early 1970s.
Photo: Tony Howard

The fact we had equipped the route and that others had added even more gear also meant it could be climbed – and enjoyed – in one to three days. So a lot of climbers had a lot of pleasure from our climb. Since the collapse of the pitches from the top, the Great Wall up to and including the Narrow Slab, when permafrost within the wall melted in 1998, it has never been repeated. Norwegian climbers who have been up to look say, 'It's hell up there.'

In 1984, Mick, Di and I teamed up with my old mate Al Baker, who I had first met when we were both dossing under the Cromlech boulders in the Llanberis Pass in 1958, for a trip to Jordan. On this occasion we hit the jackpot, discovering the mountains of Wadi Rum in south Jordan, after which I dreamed up the wheeze of n.o.m.a.d.s. – New Opportunities for Mountaineering, Adventure and Desert Sports – to enable Di and I to work as adventure travel consultants, not only with Jordan's Ministry of Tourism, but to get us to mountains elsewhere that other people couldn't reach. The idea was that in return for sponsorship and any necessary permits we could advise on any adventure tourism potential and help to publicise it, hopefully for the benefit of the local communities, as had happened in Romsdal and Rum.

We have been in Rum every year since, having established a close friendship with the local Bedouin on our first visit, something that has been of inestimable value to us and other climbers ever since. The Bedouin themselves proved to be great climbers and knew the mountains intimately having passed down knowledge of their hunting routes over the generations. These routes have been recognised by others as among the world's best desert adventures, and Rum itself as among the world's best desert-climbing areas, maybe the best. Who am I to argue? Following publication of our guide to *Treks and Climbs in Wadi Rum* we were also sponsored by Queen Noor to write a guide to *Jordan's Walks, Treks, Caves, Climbs and Canyons*, in the hope that, like the Rum guide, it would bring visitors to lesser-known and comparatively poor parts of the country. These two books have been credited with kick-starting

Jordan's now booming adventure tourism.

Under the auspices of n.o.m.a.d.s. Di and I also made trips to Libya, exploring sea cliffs, deserts and the remote Akakus mountains in the south west. In Madagascar we climbed at Tsaranoro and were allowed into the nearby Andringitra National Park, which was not yet open to visitors, trekking to the summit of Pic Boby, its highest point, on commission from a magazine. Back in the Middle East we had a marvellous three months exploring Oman and contributing to Alec MacDonald's guidebook to rock-climbing there.

One project we felt passionately about was writing the guidebook to a new trail being developed in Palestine for the millennium. The Nativity Trail, which was a Palestinian Authority project, starts in Nazareth and goes through the hills of the West Bank to Bethlehem. The route was based around the Biblical story of Joseph and Mary's journey to Bethlehem for the birth of Jesus. The idea was that the ten-day trail with its overnight stops in villages, staying in Palestinian homes, would bring walkers to Palestine to aid the economy and to experience for themselves what life was like under the Israeli occupation. But not long after finishing the project the Israeli wall was started. Not only did it cut village from village and local people from their schools, hospitals and farmland, but it, and the increasing number of Israeli checkpoints, also cut The Nativity Trail in several places, making the journey impossible. Happily in recent years the ever-resilient Palestinians have re-opened some sections that are once again being walked.

Di and I also travelled through Ethiopia, climbing Ras Dashan in the Simien Mountains and noting the climbing potential around Axum and Tigray, before hitching to tribal villages near the Omo River deep in the south. Together with friends we also had four trips to the Nubian Desert of south east Egypt with help from Egypt's Department of Tourism and a local tour operator. The first two trips were stopped by the military despite permits but we managed to get into the desert further north, locating some long forgotten climbs of the great Italian alpinist Emilio Comici.

On our third trip we were finally allowed in after a two week permit delay. Despite the loss of time, we found and climbed the remote and reputedly unclimbable dome of Gebel Sila'i, as well as the spectacular rock bridge of the Farayids, just above the coast. On our last day, we also located our third objective, the remarkable unclimbed mountain pinnacle of the Berenice Bodkin, but, with no time left, had to leave it for the following year.

We returned with the same Egyptian tour operator who had, he said, obtained the necessary permits again, but we guessed something was wrong when he avoided the checkpoints. We were subsequently arrested and after a night in custody and a thousand-mile drive back to Cairo, spent a night in military jail and then had to go to court. It turned out that the permits were last year's with altered dates. The whole area was – and still is – closed by the military. The judge accepted our ignorance of the permit situation, but the tour operator lost his licence and did time in jail. Such is life.

The Himalaya also beckoned, with a trek round the Annapurna Circuit and two trips partially sponsored by an Indian tour operator into Nagaland on the Burmese border of north east India, for which it was very difficult to obtain permits. Having failed to climb Saramati when our Naga porters disappeared on a bear hunt, we opened a trek through the jungle villages at its foot, being welcomed in one with a celebratory dance, and told we were the first strangers to visit.

After the sale of Troll in 1995, these trips became much easier. Di and I were now free spirits with no work obligations. I think I can say that the equipment designed at Troll before and after the Troll Wall climb was revolutionary and had a beneficial impact on climbing safety and therefore on standards. Yet I am even happier that our continuing climbing explorations have in many cases been of benefit not simply to the climbers and trekkers who have followed in our footsteps, or to the host countries and companies who helped sponsor our trips but, most importantly, to the mountain, jungle and desert people we met on our travels. All of them showed us only friendship, kindness and hospitality, even when we were strangers.

As a Naga chief said to us when we arrived in his village and were welcomed as guests, with people vacating their beds for us, 'We have nothing to give, but you are welcome.' Being given beans from the field of a struggling Ethiopian farmer toiling with his wooden plough, or being offered what little food was available at a poor Bedouin camp, knowing that they would go without, or being greeted by a Palestinian with the words, 'You gave away my country, but you are welcome, come and have some tea,' were humbling and salutary experiences. No refusal was ever accepted.

I thank them all here for reminding us what life and humanity is really about.

Appendix

In Praise of Madness

by Ole Daniel Enersen

TWENTY YEARS BEFORE NIKE THOUGHT OF IT, our motto was 'just do it.' The Troll Wall, Trollveggen, dark, tall and forbidding, was the dream Norwegian climbers dared not speak of. Talking to yourself, however, is something else, and for me the wall had been a dream since I first saw it in 1957 from the top of Romsdalshorn. Attacking big walls had only been done twice earlier in Norway, first in 1936 by Arne Næss on the South Pillar of Stetind in North Norway and then, in 1958, when Ralph Høibakk and Arne Randers Heen climbed the Trollryggen – the big East Pillar beside Trollveggen – from Romsdalen[1], an early warning of a new era.

At the start of the 1960s several young Norwegian climbers started to do harder routes. One of the driving forces in this development was Bjørn Halvorsen, almost twenty years older than the rest of us. In 1964 he began arranging trips to Romsdalen. This resulted in many fine climbs, with the highpoint coming in late spring of 1965, when we made the first ascent of the 1,000-foot West Wall of Romsdalshorn. 'We' were Bjørn Halvorsen, Odd Eliassen, Jon Teigland and myself.

The West Wall of Romsdalshorn, which is perched 4,000 feet above the valley floor, was awesome by the standards of the time, and because of a late start we had to bivouac on a ledge just large enough for the four of us to sit on with our stove. It was a cold night, and the topic of the night's conversation was right opposite us on the other side of the valley: the Troll Wall.

---

1 *Author's note:* Romsdalen is the correct Norwegian name for what English-speakers refer to as Romsdal. In Norway, Romsdal is a larger area going from the mountains all the way to the ocean, part of the district of Møre og Romsdal.

Nobody had ever made a serious attempt to climb it, and according to the popular press it was probably impossible. However, a saying ascribed to the Norwegian polar explorer Roald Amundsen proved true. Nothing is impossible; the impossible just takes more time.

We still had no firm plans for the wall. The decisive moment came one evening in early June while training at Kolsås, the local crag in Oslo. A Norwegian-American we had not met before, Leif Norman Patterson, arrived at Gårdsplassen, the place climbers meet and drink tea before and after climbs. Jon and I were just preparing for a new route on a big overhang, and we invited Leif to join us.

While I hammered my way through the overhang Leif told Jon that he had arrived in Norway to climb the Troll Wall, having with him all the new American big-wall equipment needed, including about 2,000 feet of rope, hardened pitons, RURPs and bongs as well as jumars. His problem, however, was that his American friends had just told him that they could not come as planned. So, a couple of hours later, when we met on the Gårdsplassen again, we had a new and pretty good idea about what to do that summer. A few days later Odd, Jon, Leif and I met and decided to go for it, and that we should go as soon as Leif had returned from a few weeks in the USA.

In late June we knew of no other teams with similar plans, but then the main Norwegian newspaper, *Aftenposten*, announced that an English team was coming. Would it be a race as the paper said? We hoped not, and it wasn't. When we met them in Romsdalen everyone was in a relaxed mood, this was no replay of Scott and Amundsen, probably to the dismay of the media.

When we started, we knew that this would probably be climbing history, but we had no idea about how big the story would become. Then again, the summer for Norwegian newspapers is a time when they lack real news, including sex and crime, and resort to stories about the biggest pumpkins. What the British call the 'silly season'. The crazy daredevils on the Troll Wall must have been a godsend for them. Every day the latest news from Romsdalen made the front page, and the police had to direct the traffic because of all the cars stopping for a glimpse of the climbers. Tourist buses also stopped, and even the trains slowed for a peep. The TV cameraman from the Norwegian Broadcasting Corporation risked his life by taking up positions at the most dangerous places under the wall. He was literally asking to get stoned, and without the need to smoke grass.

We initially tried a direct line up to the summit gully, which, as it turned out, became the upper part of the Rimmon Route, but our route became a huge waterfall after so many rainy days. Having also experienced a major stone avalanche, we decided to move our starting point further down, escaping all the water and also the falling stones, but making our route significantly longer. Our strategy was to fix ropes on the lower parts, and then go for the top when the weather was fine. That proved a good tactic, making it possible to have a trip to the cinema when the weather became too bad.

The climbing was as expected, with a combination of technical and free climbing at a high standard, with easier parts in between. Hauling gear during the final eight days was, however, worse than we thought, because we brought too much equipment, including chocolates, and problems with loose stones on ledges. We had some very long days. Between the second and third bivouacs, the climbing was one long traverse, which took Jon and I twenty two hours with all the gear. It was five in the morning when we arrived at the great ledge on the East Pillar, which was our halfway home for the next twenty six hours, a lazy day in the sun. Who said climbing was hard?

The next day Jon and I had some very difficult free climbing, exposed and with poor belays. The day after Leif and Odd came to the crucial pitch, also very exposed and on the wall itself, with poor belays. Here Odd spent five hours on seventy feet of A3. Later on, our main problem was that the two climbers in front did not have food with them, but could hear the hauling team enjoying themselves as they starved.

In spite of these experiences, the Norwegian team found climbing together so enjoyable that we tried to join forces again as soon as possible. Two years later Leif was back again from the US. Our plan was to add another new route on the Troll Wall, but after a few rope lengths an accident prevented a successful outcome.

Our contacts with the English climbers doing the Rimmon Route were also pleasant, and Jon climbed with Tony Howard, Rob Holt and another Rimmon lad, Wayne Gartside, in the spring of 1967, when they attempted the 1,500-foot North Face of Blåstolen, further down the fjord from Åndalsnes, but were turned back by loose rock, blind cracks and bad weather. Very soon we started to dream about joining forces at bigger walls, including an attempt at 'the world's biggest wall' on Nanga Parbat in the Himalaya, together with John Amatt. Later on that dream changed to doing the South West Face of Everest. This could have been achieved when Odd and Jon joined an International Everest expedition in 1971, together with Dougal Haston and Don Whillans, among others. However, the expedition was not successful. Coming back from Everest in 1971 Odd made the first Norwegian ascent of the Rimmon Route, and I followed suit in 1996, together with a 16-year-old lad.

Leif also continued big-wall climbing, but sadly died in an avalanche when coming back home from an expedition to K2. Odd, whose name means the 'tip of the arrow' in Norwegian, continued to live according to our slogan, climbing on all continents, having been on the top of Kilimanjaro at least seventy times, but on the summit of Everest only once.

'Just do it,' however, doesn't seem such an appropriate motto for our route on the Troll Wall. Several teams have tried it, but as far as we know the second ascent was not until 1997, also by Norwegians. Since then it has been repeated only two or three times.

Ole Daniel Enersen
Thanks to Jon Teigland and Odd Eliassen for comments.

Acknowledgements

I WOULD LIKE TO THANK Dave Durkan for initiating the search for Troll Wall memorabilia after the passing of forty five years since our ascent. I am also indebted to Di Taylor, my partner on and off the rocks for the last thirty years, for inspiring my writing and climbing and for unearthing the manuscript for this book from its forgotten corner on our bookshelf and encouraging me to publish it - an enthusiasm shared by Mick Shaw and Bruce Mills despite my doubts. It was at their insistence that I sent the 1965 manuscript to Ed Douglas for his opinion on its worth. Much to my surprise, having read it, he asked if he could forward it to Jon Barton of Vertebrate Graphics for his consideration – it is thanks to Ed and Jon that this book finally made it into print. It has been a pleasure to work with them. Also a special thanks to Margaret Birch (née Woodcock) and John Amatt who provided their photos of our trip. And to Di Taylor's sister, Mary, for drawing the fiendish little Trolls that enliven the headings.

Fred Husøy and many others have helped with the search for photos or provided photos. I am grateful to them all: Willy Vestå of Blådet Veserålen, Arnulf Glad, Benedikte Andreassen, Reidar Larssen, Hanne Knudsen of Innovation Norway, Madeleine Roast of Magnetic PR (magneticpr.co.uk), Gyri Midtveit of Destination Lofoten, Alf Oxem, Snorre E Aske, Sigurd Skjegstad, Bjørn Kirkhaug, Halvor Sødahl, Iver Gjelstenli, Harald Sæterøy, Rob Holt and Di Taylor. Finally a special thanks to Ole D Enersen for his photos of, and chapter on, the 1965 Norwegian Route, including the photos by the late Leif Norman Patterson, and also to two of his companions on the climb, Jon Teigland and Odd Eliassen for contributing. Finally, to Joe Brown for his kind quote, Ed Douglas for his excellent editing, Ian Smith for his proof-reading and Doug Scott for his greatly appreciated foreword.

Tony Howard, Greenfield, on the northern edge of the Peak District
January 2011

Glossary

Abseil

In 1965, this was a method of coiling the rope round the body to make a quick controlled descent, now done with considerably more comfort using a harness and specially designed 'descender'.

Arête

A steep, well-defined, rib or ridge of rock.

Aid climbing

A method of climbing using pegs and nuts for direct 'artificial aid', rather than just for protection.

Belay

A secure point at the start and end of every rope-length, or pitch, from which to 'belay' the leading or second climber in safety.

Bergschrund

A German term: the crevasse separating a snowfield from a rock wall, often very wide and deep.

Carabiners

Metal snaplinks made of steel up to the mid 1960s, but now of light alloy, usually D-shaped, with a spring gate opening in one side.

Chockstones

Anything from a pebble to a large rock jammed in a crack around which a sling can often be threaded for protection or aid. Before the use of 'nuts' in the late 1950s it was not uncommon to carry some well-chosen pebbles specifically for that purpose.

Dièdre
A French term, commonly used in the Alps, to denote a huge 'open book' corner. Usually very steep.

Etrier
A French term: lit. stirrup. A small ladder, usually of cord with three wooden or metal rungs and a loop at the top for the attachment of a carabiner or similar device. Tape etriers, which were in common use in the 1960s and often referred to simply as 'tapes' served the same purpose but are lighter, being made up of knotted loops of nylon tape.

Expansion bolt
In the 1960s this usually referred to a self-expanding bolt that could be hammered into a specially drilled hole and fitted with a metal hanger for the attachment of a carabiner to aid upwards progress. Traditionally considered a last resort for climbers.

Exposure
The psychological effect of height above the ground, to some extent reduced by running belays.

Extreme
The highest category of grading on British rock-climbs in the 1960s.

Free-climbing
Climbing in the traditional style without recourse to aid from pegs, nuts, and so on.

Hand-jam
The technique of jamming the hand into a crack, to provide a hold where no other is available.

Hardware
A term sometimes used to refer to pegs, carabiners, and so on.

Harness
At the time of the Troll Wall ascent there were no waist harnesses. The team used a specially made belt designed by the author that could also be used as a sit-harness for aid climbing and abseiling – see *Introduction*.

Ironmongery
See *Hardware*.

Nuts
In the early 1960s these were ordinary metal engineering nuts threaded onto a nylon sling, to be used for jamming into cracks instead of a peg. It was usual to carry two or three different sizes on each sling. Specially designed nuts (some designed and made by the author and friends – see *Introduction*) were beginning to take over by the time of the Troll Wall ascent.

Pegs
Metal spikes of varying lengths and dimensions for hammering into cracks, with an eyehole at the outer end for the attachment of a carabiner. They fall broadly into three types – vertical (in which the eye is in the same plane as the blade), horizontal (in which the eye is at 90° to the blade) and channel (in which the blade has a U-shaped cross section.

Pitch
The distance between two belays; anything up to a rope length, maximum 150 feet in the 1960s, though these days longer and lighter ropes – and therefore pitches – are common on big routes.

Pitons

See *Pegs*. A French term but in common use elsewhere.

Prusik

A method of climbing a rope using special equipment or techniques. Today's specialist equipment did not exist in the UK in 1965.

Serac

A large, unstable, block of snow or ice that has detached itself from the main mass.

Stance

A ledge, often small, that can be used to belay from.

Tapes

See *Etriers*.

Wedge

A wooden wedge (usually home-made) for hammering into cracks too wide for pegs. They are of various thicknesses and have a hole at the outer end, through which a loop of nylon is threaded for the attachment of a carabiner. Frequently essential for aid-climbing wide, overhanging and otherwise protectionless cracks in the 1960s, now replaced by the miracle of camming devices, the various sizes of which will expand to fit all sizes of crack from less than half an inch up to six inches.

Further reading

Tony Howard, *Climbs, Scrambles and Walks in Romsdal* (4th edn, Cordee, 2005). ISBN: 9781904207245.

Connie Roos, *Walking in Norway* (Cicerone Press, 2010). ISBN: 9781852842307.

Peter Lennon, *Scandinavian Mountains* (West Col, 1987). ISBN: 0906227321.

Anne Grete Nebell og Bjarte Bø, *Klatring I Romsdal* (Sogge Fjellsport, 1999). ISBN: 8299503205.

Iver Gjelstenli, *Fra topp til topp i Romsdal* (1997). ISBN: 8291883009.

Per Hohle, *Til Fots I Rondane-Dovrefjell-Trollheimen* (Gyldendal Norske Forlag, 1972). ISBN: 8205026254.

Anthony Dyer, John Baddeley and Ian H. Robertson, *Walks & Scrambles in Norway* (Rockbuy, 2006). ISBN: 9781904466253.

W. Cecil Slingsby, *Norway: The Northern Playground* (new edn, Rockbuy, 2003). First published 1904. ISBN: 1904466079.

John Amatt, *Straight to the Top and Beyond: Nine Keys for Meeting the Challenge of Changing Times* (Jossey Bass, 1996). ISBN: 0893842966. Available from: One Step Beyond WorldWide, Suite 200, 838 – 10th Street, Canmore, Alberta, Canada T1W 2A7
www.osbworldwide.com

Author's website
www.nomadstravel.co.uk